DARK PSYCHOLOGY

THE ART OF USING NLP, NON-VERBAL COMMUNICATIONS, BODY LANGUAGE AND PERSUASION TO GET PEOPLE TO DO WHAT YOU WANT

CHARLES CUMMINGS

PUBLISHING FORTE

Disclaimer:
Copyright © Year 2021
All Rights Reserved.

Please do not copy and distribute this book in any manner without the permission of the author. This includes emails, recordings, or other audio-visual electronic methods.

You can share this book in the manner provided by the Fair Use Laws. Fair Use exceptions include only small quotes, critical reviews, and non-commercial uses.

The purpose of this book is to inspire and motivate. If you're looking for psychiatric or psychological advice, please consult a professional.

The content of this book is the *opinion* of the author. The author does not form a client-and-service-provider relationship with the reader. Therefore, the reader may rely on the information provided in this book at their own risk.

Every piece of advice given in this book is truthful and fair. The author has made sure that the information provided is correct at the time of publication. Readers should take the author's advice at their discretion. They should understand that such advice does not replace a counselor, psychologist, or psychiatrist's professional opinion.

The author of this book does not guarantee the results for sure. Therefore, they are not liable for any physical, psychological, financial, or commercial damages. There's no assurance that what has worked for one person would work for another.

1
AN INTRODUCTION TO NLP AND DARK PSYCHOLOGY

I t's not a secret that all the successful people in the world fit the Dark Triad Model.

DARK TRIAD PERSONALITIES ARE CUT-THROAT, risk-taking, chameleon-like, ruthless personalities who candy-coat themselves with a dazzling charm and charisma.

FROM POLITICIANS and celebrities to Silicon Valley CEOs and business leaders – the Dark Triads are *everywhere*.

PSYCHOLOGISTS SAY that one in every five business leaders has Dark Triad tendencies – and we see glimpses of that statistic in the notorious Zuckerberg Stare and Donald Trump's political statements.

. . .

IN THIS BOOK, we'll be studying Dr-Jekyll-and-Mr. Hyde-esque personalities that the Dark Triad are – a branch of Psychology referred to as Dark Psychology.

DARK PSYCHOLOGY ALLOWS us to see the traits, language neutrality, and thinking patterns of Dark Triad and know why those traits are *so* successful.

AFTER WE'VE DONE THAT, we'll apply those traits to our personal lives using a technique called Neuro-Linguistic Programming (NLP). NLP is simply a study and mimicking of certain people's language, actions, and thinking patterns. In the end, you will be likely to master the art of persuasion and achieve your goals by convincing and swaying others.

Dark Psychology

Dark Psychology is simply a study of the tactics that many people employ to harm others. These include patterns of manipulation, coercion, lying, and other means of influence. Besides that, it also seeks to understand the thoughts, emotions, and perceptions behind predatory behavior against others.

DARK PSYCHOLOGY STATES that most of this behavior and the purposeful victimization of others is guided by malicious intent or with some kind of ulterior motive 99% of the time. However, it also believes that 1% of such behaviors may have no purposive intent or be accounted for by science or religious dogma. This is something that truly sets Dark Psychology apart from other behavioral studies and forms of Psychology; it believes that there is a small segment of our population that does not commit heinous acts for money, sex, power, or retribution, but rather without any goal or motive. They do it because of the sake of doing so, simply because they can. Theories within this field of the study state that exploring such a side in individuals is incredibly complex and even more difficult to define.

DARK PSYCHOLOGY POSITS that all humans are on a continuum of malicious and evil acts, wherein some people might be more prone to committing harmful acts than others. Some might just have obtrusive thoughts, while others *will* act on these thoughts and commit deviant crimes against others. This is also known as the **Dark Continuum**. Those benevolent amongst us would have lower rates of these thoughts and urges, but the same cannot be sad about the few evil ones amongst us. Hence predicting who commits these deviant crimes is difficult, according to Dark Psychology. This dark side in individuals is unpredictable and can exist in anyone regardless of their religion, culture, geographical location, and whatnot.

DESPITE THOSE OF us who'd instead not think of how dark humanity can be, there *are* people in the world who have dedicated their lives to studying precisely that. They study to understand the intent behind these behaviors and what drives them, the social and biological factors contributing to their psyche, and more.

SOME OF THE other things that Dark-Psychology researchers study include:

- Identifying emotionally manipulative traits

- Recognizing individual behaviors
- Predicting dangerous or harmful acts of manipulative people
- Creating profiles for law enforcement

Dark Psychology has captured the attention of millions of people worldwide, and the information that it can provide is indispensable to both health and justice. It's also an entertainment genre of its own. It is the subject of some of the most high-quality, super-informative fictional and real-crime shows, podcasts, YouTube channels, and documentaries. Think about the amount of TV shows and movies you've come across that highlight the thinking patterns and behaviors of the world's most notorious serial killers, sociopaths, and psychopaths.

WHILE PSYCHOLOGY DIGS into an *individual*'s thoughts, actions, feelings, and relationships, Dark Psychology digs into the darker tactics that certain people use to get what they want and to victimize others. While psychology studies the emotions, thoughts, and behaviors in our everyday reactions, Dark Psychology dives into the human mind's hidden and darker parts. It covers why people influence each other, how they do it, and the common tactics globally used. So, in other words, Dark Psychology aims to uncover the concealed parts of our identities and digs deeper into the human psyche. It explores the criminal and deviant behaviors that guide the often unlawful actions as well. But this is not to say that Dark Psychology exists only within killers; these manipulators can well and truly be amongst us and not exactly have motives to murder or steal. The main aim of such individuals is to prey upon others, and they typically don't have any moral or empathetic grounds to guide their behaviors.

. . .

THESE TACTICS ARE USED DIFFERENTLY, depending on the setting, whether it's a workplace, a parent-child relationship, or an intimate relationship. These 'dark' tactics that people use include:

- Manipulation
- Guilt Tripping
- Seduction
- Subliminal Messages
- Lying
- Love Bombing

and more that we will be studying in-depth in the next few chapters.

IN SOCIAL SETTINGS that involve close relationships, Dark Psychology can be defined as using a set of techniques to manipulate others to get them to do something which may not be of benefit to them exactly, but would benefit the manipulator. This is much different from persuasion, and we will be talking in great detail about the difference between persuasion and manipulation. This field of study can also be used in intimate relationships to manipulate someone in order to satisfy one's own sexual strategies. Someone with Dark Psychology tendencies is in a relationship with someone without complete and honest regard for that person and only seeks to satisfy their own needs and urges and to control the other person. This can include outright abuse, jealous behaviors, devaluation, lowering the other person's self-esteem, and more that we shall discuss in the upcoming sections.

. . .

DARK PSYCHOLOGY STARTED BECOMING popular in the early 2000s when cybercriminals began gathering knowledge on criminal psychology and predicting where the subsequent cyber attacks would occur. They would stalk, coerce, blackmail, and exploit people that they find online using the information and knowledge on criminal psychology. Most of them are sexual predators, pedophiles, cyber terrorists, cyber bullies, and more.

HOWEVER, research in the field of Dark Psychology has existed for decades before and has led to some of the judicial field's most incredible developments. Criminal profiling has armed law-enforcement and law-implementing authorities alike with a weapon that helps them catch criminals, predict their next target, and prevent crimes from happening. Old-school laws are made more efficient now that they're made, keeping in mind the most malicious actions amongst us.

MORE THAN ANYTHING ELSE, Dark Psychology's growing popularity has forced even the strongest nay-sayers to open their eyes and notice the darkest sides of human nature. There are dark traits in the most optimistic of all people. Human beings are a complex amalgamation of emotions, thoughts, actions, and temperament – and Dark Psychology attempts to answer all of those questions backed with research and studies.

What Dark Psychology *isn't*

There are some people who have many misconceptions about Dark Psychology and myths surrounding this field of study. Here we dispel some of the most common myths:

- It's not hypnosis – everyone that's involved is in their full senses!
- It's not psychopathy – Many psychopaths use Dark Psychology, many don't.
- It's not brainwashing– again, everyone that's involved is in their full senses.

Many people believe that Dark Psychology involves hypnosis and mind control; that is simply not true. Of course, there are great levels of persuasion involved, but you are not controlling anyone's mind. People are in their full senses when they make a decision influenced by you. The same applies to brainwashing; Dark Psychology is definitely not complete control of an individual to get them to do or believe in what you want them to. Everyone is in their full senses at all times.

Moreover, Dark Psychology is not psychopathy either. Psychopathy is a mental disease. There are some psychopaths who use this field of study, but many that don't. Dark Psychology involves all humans and is not just limited to a certain set of people. Like we said, we all engage in 'dark' thoughts and even behaviors from time to time. Hence this field of study is not just limited to psychopaths but rather to all humans.

We'll be getting into the nitty-gritty of all of these tactics in Chapter Two of the book.

Dark Psychology Traits

In Dark Psychology, the personality traits that fall under the typical behavior of manipulators are known as the 'Dark Triad.'

These are those individuals that have malevolent, cruel, and evil qualities. They may be difficult to deal with and have a combination of toxic traits. Those who have the Dark Psychology traits may fall under the Dark Triad and commit crimes, cause others distress, and create considerable amounts of problems in society.

Though these Dark Triad personalities may have common qualities and appear to be overlapping, they are distinct from one another.

The Dark Triad

These certain kinds of people that use shady tactics are called the Dark Triad Personalities. There are three of them.

Narcissism

Individuals who might be high on narcissism possess a mix of traits that include grandiosity, dominance, entitlement, egotistical, superiority, and lack of empathy. They are full of themselves and only think of their gain and benefit. Individuals who appear to be narcissists can also be diagnosed as having Narcissistic Personality Disorder (NPD). These narcissists can become emotionally abusive and even violent when they believe that they are not receiving the attention and recognition they deserve.

Narcissists can be either grandiosely narcissistic or vulnerably narcissistic. The two are quite unique from each other because grandiosely narcissistic individuals engage in exhibitionism, lack of modesty, and dominance over others. On the other hand, vulnerably narcissistic individuals would experience negative affect, have a hard time trusting others, be selfish, and have a profound need for validation and attention from others.

Psychopathy

This refers to a lack of emotional responses, including empathy and remorse. Out of the three personalities in the Dark Triad, this one is considered to be the most harmful, dark, and malevolent. They have the potential to cause more harm to society as compared to narcissists and those with the Machiavelli trait.

Being a psychopath is *not* a mental health disorder but rather a personality trait. In the DSM, psychopaths can be characterized as having an antisocial personality disorder. They also tend to have high levels of impulsivity and thrill-seeking behavior and can be manipulative, emotionally abusive, and volatile.

Machiavellianism

People with this personality trait are *very* goal-oriented. They will manipulate, deceive, trick, and exploit others to get what they want and achieve their goals. Individuals with this personality trait believe that it is okay to be cruel, deceitful, and cold in order to succeed and thus act accordingly. Additionally, they are likely to not have any morals or principles guiding their behaviors.

It is important to note that Machiavellianism is not a mental health diagnosis but rather describes a personality trait. Of the three personalities in the Dark Triad, this one is considered to be the one linked mostly with high intelligence. Moreover, Machiavellianism is also correlated with psychopathology, meaning that the two can exist in one person.

Additional Traits of Dark Psychology

The Dark Triad aren't the only personality traits that reflect the darker sides of human nature. There are several more to the mix markers of malignancy and use people around them intentionally and unintentionally.

THESE INCLUDE:

- Having an overly sensitive ego.
- An inflated sense of self.
- A belief that they're entitled to special treatment.
- A high degree of moral disengagement.
- Sadistic tendencies.
- A spiteful nature.

People who exhibit dark psychology traits are willing to cause harm to other people, even if it means that they harm their own selves in the process – this is their spiteful nature at play. They also engage in sadistic behaviors, where they derive pleasure from causing physical and emotional harm to other people. This gives them a sense of control and power over their victims, a major driving force for these personality types. Additionally, these people don't subscribe to a specific morality - they are known for thinking of themselves as above and beyond society's regular norms and rules. This is because they feel zero sense of guilt. In fact, they get away doing all sorts of unethical things because they cannot feel shame or guilt after the fact.

THEIR SENSE of entitlement is where it gets horrifying. They honestly, genuinely believe that they deserve everyone else's time, money, respect, and resources. When denied, their more authentic, darker selves start to pop out and become aggressive and even violent. Their inflated sense of self prevents them from working effectively in team or group environments because they want to exert power – which is why they're attracted to leadership roles like politicians, priests, and law enforcement to exercise their control over vulnerable people. They also determine their self-worth based on what other people think of them and are incredibly fragile when people don't give them the attention and praise they think they deserve.

IT'S ALSO helpful to keep in mind that having just one of these traits isn't enough for someone to be labeled a dark personality. Truly dark people, like hardened criminals, exhibit a complex multiple of all these traits, some to a greater extent than others. They also tend to be highly intelligent individuals who know what to say and when. For that reason, they are really good at concealing their true identities. Most of them are also charming, gregarious, and nice, but it is all a façade for the darkness that they hide within themselves.

SOMETIMES, these traits are very profession-specific, as well. Many workplaces and professional fields *reward* Dark Psychology traits. There are some professions where such individuals truly thrive and succeed.

. . .

THESE INCLUDE:

- Lawyers
- Public Speakers
- Politicians
- Salespersons
- CEOs
- Surgeons
- Police Officers

and more. We'll be getting to that in subsequent chapters of this book as well.

How Do Dark Psychology Traits Manifest?

All of the traits we just talked about manifest themselves in a number of different ways, including socially, sexually, virtually, emotionally, and physically.

YOU'LL SEE these traits manifest in **social** settings, like when you're on a date, hanging out with friends, or playing catch with coworkers. Suddenly, they'll be too physically close despite you pulling away because they want to create a false sense of comfort. The friendly game of catch is all of a sudden too competitive because of their inflated egos. They want to win everything, no matter how petty. They want conversations to be about them. When the conversation and attention are not on them, they can get agitated and frustrated. They exert full dominance over the entire room in a get-together with their loudness.

. . .

NOT ONLY THAT, but you'll also see predatory social behavior at the workplace and in personal and romantic encounters. These traits manifest sexually when the dark personality type targets vulnerable children, earns their trust, grooms them, and abuses them. However, sexually predatory behavior isn't just limited to children; people of any gender and race may fall victim to this form of manifestation of dark psychology. Even individuals who find themselves in a relationship with someone with the Dark Triad personality traits are coerced and seduced by them. They might be forced to engage in sexual acts they don't consent to, and more often than not, hold a submissive position in such instances, whether they want to or not.

ANOTHER WAY that dark psychology traits can manifest is through **virtual** or online predatory behaviors. These include using technology, social media, dating websites, and various other tools to commit virtual scams. Social media allows people to craft multiple identities within a matter of minutes and communicate with anyone across the world. People have scammed millions off of others using digital platforms, resulting in significant financial losses. They may also use the internet to lure people into their trap of predatory behavior, con them into believing that they are genuinely nice and once they are fooled, take advantage of them.

THIS BEHAVIOR MANIFESTS **emotionally** as well; here, the hunting ground is intimate relationships. By personal relationships, we mean the relationships between relatives, parents, close friends, and partners. These relationships require us to be emotionally vulnerable, narrate our deepest fears, our darkest secrets, share the most intimate everyday details of our lives, and much more. If you have a predator in these circles, none of your private parties are safe; they *will* be used against you. It's harrowing to be manipulated by those closest to you and can take a lifelong toll on your emotional health.

NOT ONLY THAT, it can become a never-ending cycle because leaving can sometimes seem like a nonexistent option. They exert so much dominance over you that being in a submissive position becomes your second nature. It will always be about them, and when they notice you slipping away, narcissists can use their charm to lure you back in. Even if you leave someone with a Dark Triad personality, they are likely to never leave you. They can go to great lengths to have you back and keep you in their lives, for example, by stalking you, manipulating, and using psychological torment.

ONE OF THE most dangerous manifestations of these personality types is when they engage in **physical abuse**. Their behavior manifests as violent and aggressive energy because of their lack of emotional control: most domestic abuse cases happen because of these dysfunctional emotional regulation modes. The fact that they don't have any emotional remorse also makes things worse because it means that the harm they can do can even be life-threatening. When their dominance is threatened, it can help truly anger individuals with Dark Triad personality traits. Moreover, it's believed that individuals in intimate relationships with them are at the most risk of being at the receiving end of their abuse.

How To Spot a Manipulator?

It's easy to identify a manipulator when you're aware of who they are, why they do what they do, and what their most common tactics look like. That is why it's important to study and be aware of how they manifest themselves and potentially exploit and manipulate you.

WHATEVER THE NATURE of your relationship with a manipulator is, every single type of relationship involves a give or take. But this transaction aims to benefit both parties and is healthy. However, it is likely that the manipulator deliberately attempts to create an imbalance of power in your relationship so that they always gain more benefit compared to you. This means that you would be the one giving more and taking less.

SOME OF THE most prolific and easy-to-recognize traits in predatory people involve:

- They'll fake emotions that they don't feel, and their expressions and gestures are exaggerated.
- They'll constantly play the victim, especially around compassionate people
- They will evade responsibility because of their inflated sense of self
- They'll hide behind other people and carefully crafted social media profiles
- They're too calm under high-stress situations
- They will look for your weaknesses and use them against you
- Through their elaborate tactics, they will make you give up something you value to serve their own benefit
- Once they are successful at manipulating you, they are likely to continue that behavior until you put an end to it

When it comes to relationships with manipulators, whether your relationship is that of friends, a parent-child one, or partners, there are sure signs of manipulation that sometimes go unnoticed because you're so used to them. Here we highlight what these are:

- They may make you undermine your grasp of reality by planting false memories or altering reality – this might end up making you question your sanity
- They will mold your perceptions as they see fit. For example, they may tell you things you want to hear, but their actions tell a completely different story
- Manipulators are excellent at making you feel guilty for anything that you do, for sharing your feelings, behaving a certain way, or even for withholding your feelings. They are masters at guilt-tripping
- They will never take accountability for their actions and always blame others for their problems and shortcomings
- They take no time in becoming intimate and close; sharing too much information too soon, and expecting the same from others
- They create an environment and dynamic in relationships wherein the other person gets sucked into the manipulator's bad moods and feels responsible for fixing it
- Manipulators will always one-up you – their problems will always be more serious
- They know what makes you nervous, angry, or upset, and they will use it against you

In the end, it's safe to say that manipulators end up driving you crazy, making you believe that your reality is flawed, that they truly are the victim in most scenarios, and that they deserve special treatment from you. But make no mistake, because it's all a ruse. To get out of the trap of manipulators is to recognize their toxic traits and habits.

YOU DON'T NEED to respond to manipulators and fulfill their needs when yours aren't even being considered. Look at the facts and begin distancing yourself from them. Set boundaries and decide where you draw the line and want out of the relationship. Once you've identified a manipulator, predicting their next move becomes easier. This is how you can play them at their own game and come out as the winner.

Neuro-Linguistic Programming (NLP)

Neuro-Linguistic Programming is a psychological tactic in which we break down the personality traits of successful people and apply them to our own lives to achieve a personal goal. We take a close look at their thoughts, language, and patterns of behavior and try to emulate them to successfully achieve a certain goal.

WE CAN BREAK down people's personality traits by looking at their language, actions, and thoughts – yes, knowing someone's thoughts is possible, especially if it is a Dark Triad Personality. The key elements that make up the theory of NLP are effective communication, modeling, and action. The main premise of the theory is that if we can understand what courses of action an individual takes to successfully accomplish a task, we can copy those actions and gain success as well. Proponents of this theory believe that the mind and body influence one another, and each sense of our body is vital in the practice of NLP. The entire process of NLP has to do with physical experience, mainly pertaining to the senses of olfactory, auditory, visual, kinesthetic, and gustatory. Therefore, since each individual differs in their experiences and perceptions, the process of NLP is unique to everyone. Moreover, it is important to note that NLP is not hypnotherapy. It works by consciously approaching thoughts, behaviors, and emotions in order to modify them.

NLP HAS its basis in the Psychology of Communication or Language. The founders of NLP are John Grinder and Richard Bandler, and they theorized that specific communication tactics make success more likely.

NLP USED theories from renowned professionals like Noam Chomsky, Alfred Korzybski, and Gregory Bateson to back up their claims.

NLP HAS ONLY BEEN around since the 1970s and is a *very* new approach to language and communication. The theory became popular when Grinder and Bandler began marketing it as a tool to achieve success through observing the behavior of successful people. However, now, the theory is used for much more than that. It is currently used in all kinds of fields – whether it's medicine, law, art, sports, performing arts, or even the military.

NLP HAS BEEN USED in the psychology field to treat a wide range of mental issues like anxiety, phobias, PTSD, depression, ADHD, borderline personality disorders, addictions, OCD, and Schizophrenia. In fact, NLP is a popular form of therapy for mental health issues. It focuses on helping such individuals to clarify their distorted and limited perspectives about life, relationships, and oneself ultimately to reach their treatment goals. NLP therapists focus on understanding their client's emotions, behaviors, and thinking patterns as well and aim to fix them.

NLP and the Six Levels of Change Model

NLP works its charm by focusing on change at six core logical levels. It's an excellent model to help individuals understand why things happen when they do and what one can do about them. This level of change model was created by Robert Dilts and Todd Epstein, who was inspired by the researchers who came up with NLP.

THIS MODEL STATES THAT PROBLEM-SOLVING, communication, change, and learning; all occur at six distinct levels.

- **Finding your purpose**

This is the highest level of the model and deals with the biggest existential question out there – what is the purpose I serve in this life? Therefore, this level involves finding the meaning of life, finding happiness, and a sense of mission. Additionally, it helps an individual figure out what greater good they serve in this world, what morals they want to follow, and whatnot. Hence this level greatly concerns religion and other related systems.

- **Finding Your Identity**

The second level aims to figure out who the individual is and what their core values, beliefs, responsibilities, and roles are. It deals with how one perceives oneself and can include asking oneself questions like who they are, how they think of themselves, what values they stand for, what their vision in life is, how others would describe them, and more.

- **Finding Your Values and Beliefs**

Closely relating to the second level is the third level, but it mainly focuses on the individual's belief system and what values they ascribe to. Our beliefs and values are the primary factors that drive our actions and thus have a huge impact on the outcomes. They also contribute to our personal identities. Yet, despite their extreme importance in our lives, we sometimes are unaware of what they actually are. To tap into this area of our consciousness, we can ask ourselves what we find right and wrong, what exact values we believe in, and why.

- **Knowing Your Skills and Capabilities**

This level is about understanding the strengths, skills, capabilities, talents, and competencies we have which influence our behaviors and actions. Ask yourself, what are the current skills and capabilities do you possess in order to make the change you want? Which skills do you not possess but need to learn in order to make this desired change?

- **Knowing Your Behaviors**

This relates to the actions of an individual generally life and also in specific situations. To tap into this level of change, there are a number of questions you can ask yourself. How do you react in a certain situation? What physical signs do you exhibit in terms of your body language, expressions, and voice when performing an action? What is your current lifestyle like? Are there any specific patterns of behavior do you follow? And are these patterns healthy or toxic?

- Knowing Your Environment

The last and lowest level in the hierarchy of levels of change has to do with your physical and social environment. This pertains to the settings we find ourselves in and the people we surround ourselves with. For example, our community, who we live with, the culture and society we are part of, our available resources, and who we spend the most amount of time with. To tap into this level of the model, you can ask the following questions: How does my environment help me meet my goals? What opportunities and hindrances do I currently face? What are the kinds of people I like to surround myself with? What are my available resources? How does my working environment make me feel? Where do I get the most support from?

NLP IS A HIGHLY individualized process because everyone's purpose, identity, values, skills, behaviors, and environment are all *very* different –even if they're twins!

NLP IS ALSO A VERY immersive process because it requires you to sit down with your feelings and past and self-reflect deeply. It entirely comes down to you and how you perceive yourself and everything around you. Hence, honest and thorough self-reflection becomes necessary when practicing NLP.

SOME COMMON NLP tactics that we can use to learn about the Dark Psychology Traits include:

- Speech recognition – how do these people talk to different kinds of people? What tone do they use?
- Word Recognition – what kinds of vocabulary are these people using?
- Affirmations, belief changes, and mental rehearsal – Introspect on what's stopping you from getting what you want, and change it.
- Value Rules – discover your values via value exercises

....and more!

WITH THE RIGHT NLP TECHNIQUES, you'll be able to model the behaviors and language patterns that enable successful people to get what they want – and eventually, you can use those tactics for personal gains as well.

Summary

In this book, we'll be teaching you:

- **What's The Secret To Certain People's Success?** You'll learn everything you need to know about what makes certain personalities more successful and more likely to get what they want.
- **How To Incorporate Those Habits into Your Own Life:** Here, we'll teach you all the different NLP tactics that you'll need to include the traits of successful personalities into your life so that you can achieve your goals and succeed as well.

By the end of this book, you'll know how to use your words, actions, and body language to get people to do what *you* want!

. . .

We've already discussed the details of what is and what dark psychology isn't in the previous chapter.

But a quick summary would be that dark psychology is the study of the shady tactics and techniques used by individuals who might fall under the dark triad.

- **Dark Tactics:** It's the study of emotionally coercive and manipulative tactics people use to get what they want and benefit themselves. It may also involve harming others for personal gain.
- **Dark Triad:** It's the study of the *people* and personality types that regularly employ those tactics. These individuals tend to fall under the personality traits of narcissists, psychopaths, and Machiavellianism.

In this second chapter of the book, we'll be deep-diving into the world of shady tactics, the dark triad, and how they constitute dark psychology.

2
DARK PSYCHOLOGY: DARK TACTICS AND DARK TRIAD

The Dark Triad is a personality model that was presented by researchers Delroy and McHoskey.
It consists of three groups of personalities that overlap with one another, namely:

- Narcissism
- Machiavellianism
- Psychopathy

These three traits are collectively called the Dark Triad. It's named so because of their high conflict, super malicious qualities of the three personalities. People scoring high on these traits are un-empathic, disagreeable, manipulative, callous, impulsive, and more likely to commit crimes than the rest of us.

THESE PERSONALITY TYPES are distinct on their own, but there's enough evidence to suggest that they overlap. This means that an individual may have traits that are common in two or all three of these personality types.

RESEARCHERS WHO STUDIED the Dark Triad believed that *all* of us have a little bit of the Dark Triad in us; we *need* it to get through the system. As we mentioned in the first chapter, researchers state that the Dark Triad personality traits exist in all of us on a scale, also known as the Dark Continuum. It's the excessive presence of these traits that becomes problematic and antagonistic.

THESE THREE PERSONALITY traits have found covert – and sometimes very overt – ways to do whatever they want and get away with it without facing any repercussions.

WE NEED to look at what the Dark Triad does and how they do it if we wish to apply it to ourselves and before using NLP to incorporate them into our lives.

REMEMBER, NLP only works if we know the tactics that we're going to be applying. This is why it is imperative to take a thorough look into all the techniques individuals of the Dark Triad use to influence others and strategically achieve their goals.

SO LET'S get started with the first of the Dark Triad.

Narcissism

The word narcissism has originated from Greek Mythology about a man named Narcissus, who fell in love with his own reflection in a pool of water and drowned in it.

. . .

ACCORDING TO RESEARCH, narcissism has the following core traits

- They're arrogant and think of themselves as superior, despite not having any achievements to warrant it
- They are attracted to positions of power
- They're entitled and exploit people to gratify their entitlement
- They always put themselves first
- Have an exaggerated sense of self-importance
- Be envious of others and believe that they are envied by others
- Have feelings of shame and insecurity, but never share it

Narcissists are of two kinds: grandiose and vulnerable. The Grandiose narcissist is a very high-conflict personality with aggression and dominance on full display. Alternatively, a Vulnerable narcissist is a very covert personality that expresses feelings through withdrawal, avoidance, and defensiveness. He is also vary of others and has a hard time trusting them.

WHERE A GRANDIOSE NARCISSIST operates on attack mode, the vulnerable narcissist operates on defense mode. Usually, the grandiose and vulnerable narcissists co-exist within the same person.

AT THEIR CORE, both kinds are still entitled, think of themselves as superior, and exploit people to get what they want. They will still think of themselves before others and demand attention on themselves at all times. Both types exhibit a lack of empathy and remorse for others, and they both have very fragile self-esteem.

A Narcissist Keeps You Stuck in Loops

Now that we have understood who a narcissist is, here's a rundown of how a narcissistic relationship usually works:

- Narcissistic people target vulnerable people and note their shortcomings
- They make the vulnerable people feel special to gain access to them
- They maintain a constant state of conflict and confusion by gaslighting, playing games, and being hot and cold
- They may alter the reality of the victim by making them believe in false memories
- When the victim decides they've had enough, the narcissist uses tactics like love bombing and hoovering to trick the person into staying
- Rinse and repeat

A narcissist sees their victim as a source of supply and uses them for validation, approval, attention, admiration, and applause. To a narcissist, their need for validation and attention is like air. When you cut their supply, you're essentially cutting off their emotional equivalent of oxygen; and they'll do *anything* to get that back. For them, a relationship is not a give or take; it is rather just take, take, and more take.

. . .

A NARCISSISTIC PARTNER may value you only because you're very attractive –simply because that makes them look good to other people. And the moment you gain a little weight, or get older, or don't wear certain kinds of clothes, you're cutting off the narcissist's supply. At this point, you might be guilt-tripped or manipulated by your partner into being 'attractive' again.

IT'S an endless cycle that takes years and sometimes decades to get out of. This is because even if you leave the narcissistic partner, they don't leave you. They may emotionally manipulate you and coerce you into returning to them by using fake emotions and words.

IT'S important to recognize and understand these tactics and how a narcissist uses them. Only then will we be able to apply NLP and incorporate them into our own lives.

Machiavellianism

A Machiavellian is someone so focused on their goal that they will do anything – including manipulating, lying, deceiving, and exploiting people – to get there.

THE TERM 'MACHIAVELLIANISM' is taken from an infamous Renaissance diplomat and philosopher named Niccolo Machiavelli. In his book 'The Prince,' Machiavelli wrote that rulers can be cruel to anyone who might be a threat to their land and that every brutal and immoral act is justifiable if the end goal is a kingdom's safety. Today, at the core of every right-wing politician's speech is Machiavellianism.

. . .

The term remained political until the 16th century when Richard Christie and Florence L. Geis developed a "Machiavellianism Scale" or the Mach-IV test. A cluster of traits was identified as Machiavellian traits, and 100 questions were asked on the test as markers of those traits. People scoring higher than 60 were called High Machs, while those scoring below were called Low Machs.

Here is a list of a few of the traits included in the test

- They're very goal-focused
- They lack empathy
- They're very charming and charismatic
- They have low interpersonal intelligence
- They lie and deceive to get what they want
- They engage in admiration and attention-seeking behaviors
- They seek prestige and status
- They're secretly cold and calculating towards other people
- They might struggle to identify their own feelings

All of us lie occasionally, but we also often feel bad – *none* of the Dark Triad personalities feels guilty over what they do. Machiavellians lack moral consciousness as well as the ability to empathize with people. They cannot engage in steady relationships with other people, so they end up using them as stepping stones on their status-seeking hikes. For them, the end goal is success.

Some of the common traits those with Machiavellianism are believed to have include

- Being charismatic and confident
- Prioritize money, power, and success over people and relationships
- Lack of values and morals
- Use flattery to get ahead
- Barely ever reveal their true intentions
- Can come across as aloof and hard to truly understand and know
- Sometimes being unaware of the consequences of their actions

Psychopathy

This is the TV show favorite of all the three Dark Triad personalities. Think *The Silence of the Lambs, American Psycho, Hannibal Lector, Dexter,* and various other depictions of psychopathic serial killers who are cold, calculating, inhuman murder machines. Many documentaries have been made just from one-on-one interviews with psychopaths.

PSYCHOPATHS ARE different from the other two of the Dark Triad in their ability to feel a very shallow range of all human emotions. They're born with psychological differences that keep them from feeling the normal range of human emotions. Not to say that they don't feel joy or rage – it just takes something deeply disconcerting, like mass murder, for them to get to that threshold. In fact, that's probably why they're impulsive and violent; they're continually searching for an excuse to feel something.

PSYCHOPATHS ARE DECEITFUL, impulsive, don't follow the law, lack empathy, and are extraordinarily egocentric and grandiose.

They're exquisite liars and have no problem clearing lie-detection tests, which test for *human* emotions that they don't have. This also makes them master manipulators. Psychopaths can be murderers, sexual predators, and even politicians.

ARGUABLY, psychopathy is the most dangerous and darkest of the three Dark Triad personalities because of their utter lack of remorse. Narcissists and Machiavellianism still experience a superficial sense of guilt and remorse, they can even show vulnerability, but psychopaths are pretty hollow in that sense. Lack of remorse means that the person would have zero sense of the consequences for their actions, which is why most serial killers, school shooters, hardened criminals, and terrorists are psychopathic. Those psychopaths who kill and murder do not have any regret or guilt over their actions but can be excellent manipulators and would even fool others to believe that they show remorse. In reality, these individuals lack any emotions ever since childhood and thus do not also have any meaningful relationships either.

OF COURSE, psychopaths also lack a moral compass. They are not driven by any principles or values. Moreover, psychopaths are also likely to be diagnosed with antisocial personality disorder, a mental health condition that describes individuals who constantly break the rules and lack empathy or remorse. However, only a small percentage of those with antisocial personality disorder can be termed psychopaths.

SOME OF THE common traits amongst psychopaths include

- Lack of guilt for their actions

- Have narcissistic tendencies
- Be superficial and charming
- Have unemotional traits

Don't confuse a sociopath with a psychopath, by the way. Although these terms are interchangeably used, they are different personality types altogether. Sociopaths are closer to Machiavellianism in the sense that they're both created by a mix of genetics and social settings. They harm an entire society. In contrast, psychopaths are the way that they are since they're toddlers. If you know someone who was a good kid until they got mixed with the wrong gang', you're dealing with a sociopath. Moreover, psychopaths tend to be more calm and calculated compared to a sociopath. They carefully plan their steps and use aggression only when needed to get what they want. However, the same cannot be said about sociopaths.

The Differences Among Narcissism, Machiavellianism, and Psychopathy

If we were to draw a Venn Diagram of the Dark Triad's traits, there'd be significant overlap. These three share a lot of core traits, for example, lack of empathy, exerting dominance and believing they are superior. However, all of these personalities are distinct on their own as well.

MACHIAVELLIANISM USES other people to do what you want. It's a personality type that focuses solely on personal gains. Other people are simple steps on their ladder to the top; manipulate them or exert power over them is part and parcel of the game. They believe that is how they will reach their goals, so they show no guilt of *using* others as stepping stones for success.

. . .

NARCISSISM, on the other hand, has traits like grandiosity, entitlement, dominance, and superiority. These people actively seek out their supply and believe they *deserve* to be continuously admired and treated differently. And when they don't, they can be hostile and even violent. For narcissists, validation and recognition are necessary aspects of survival.

PSYCHOPATHY IS SIMPLY shallow emotions or lack thereof. It's different from narcissism because, at their core, narcissists are deeply insecure and super anxious. Narcissists and those with Machiavellian traits can feel slight remorse or guilt, but that is not the case in psychopathy. Psychopaths have fewer emotions, low anxiety, super cold, and calculating. They think about each of their next steps and can even fake their emotions if they need to. Additionally, psychopaths are born, whereas Machiavellian traits or Narcissism are more or less nurtured and learned through upbringing.

ALL IN ALL, each of the three personality traits can be differentiated from one another. It is possible that an individual exhibits signs of each or two of these, but there will be specific features that will serve as distinctions. Either way, these individuals can be dangerous once allowed in your inner circle. This is because they can have a detrimental impact on your mental and sometimes even physical wellbeing.

Identifying Individuals with Dark Triad Personalities

The Dark Triad personalities aren't the only ones who exhibit traits of dark psychology. All the three traits of the Dark Triad exhibit *some* use of the tactics we study in Dark Psychology, but many don't.

. . .

INDIVIDUALS with the Dark Triad personalities can quite easily conceal their true personalities and manipulate others to believe that they are not malevolent or evil. For example, narcissists can have a positive first impression by being pleasant and amiable. This is probably because they display their high self-esteem, which is a socially desirable trait. You might find yourself charmed by narcissists when you first meet them. However, with time, as you grow closer, they may disclose their true selves by becoming manipulative and emotionally abusive.

THE SAME APPLIES to those with Machiavellian and Psychopathic tendencies. These individuals from the Dark Triad are master manipulators, and they can make you believe and do what they want quite easily. Hence, concealing their intentions and feelings is second nature to them.

LUCKILY, there are non-verbal and behavioral cues that can help researchers and others identify individuals with the Dark Triad traits. Webster also devised a test with twelve items; this test is known as the 'Dirty Dozen.' It aims to find out if an individual falls under any of the three personality traits described in the Dark Triad. The higher their score, the more likely it is for them to fall in the triad.

THE DIRTY DOZEN test provides a series of statements that individuals have to rate their agreeableness with. These statements are:

- I tend to manipulate others to get what I want
- I have used deceit or lies to get what I want
- I have used flattery to get my way
- I tend to exploit others for my benefit
- I tend to lack emotional remorse
- I tend to not be too concerned with morality or the morality of my actions
- I tend to be callous or insensitive
- I tend to be cynical
- I tend to want others to admire me
- I tend to want others to pay attention to me
- I tend to seek prestige or status
- I tend to expect special favors from others

The Dark Triad's Tricks and Manipulations

The Dark Triad engages in a variety of tricks and manipulative tactics to get what they want. Some of these tricks are so well thought out and covert that you probably don't even notice them happening. Or maybe they engage in these manipulations so often in their lives that it becomes their second nature and reflexive response. Either way, it is detrimental to the wellbeing of the individuals who are being manipulated by them. These individuals who have been around Dark Triad personalities become desensitized to their manipulations, which is why it is important to take a closer look into each of these tricks in order to identify them. We can get easily played and controlled at the hands of manipulators and may even have an uneasy feeling in our gut about them. Yet, our guilt takes the best of us, and we ignore these feelings.

IT IS essential to know exactly what you're dealing with if you suspect being in a relationship with a potential manipulator.

This will allow you to strategically approach their covert manipulations and set boundaries for yourself. In the next section of this chapter, we'll give you a rundown of the major tricks used by manipulators.

A SIDE NOTE: Every time we use the word 'relationships,' we mean dynamics between two people that could be romantic, professional, platonic, and familial.

Gaslighting:

In simple terms, when someone questions your reality and makes you doubt yourself, they're gaslighting you.

THE TERM COMES from a play called *Gaslight*, in which a sadistic husband is regularly playing games with his wife. In one event, he turns the oil lamps on and off, and upon his wife insisting that he stop, the husband denies doing anything in the first place. Slowly and surely, the wife is driven mad because she'd lost her sense of reality.

ALL OF US are guilty of doing it to one another every time we ask the question, "Are you sure?" But most of us do it unconsciously and are apologetic for it. With the dark triad personalities, it's deliberate. They might cleverly question you on whether the abuse or manipulation actually happened when you confront them about it, thus confusing you and making you doubt your reality, perception, and memory.

. . .

Some gaslight-y phrases or techniques that manipulative people might have used on you, or you may have used one someone else include:

- Telling someone they're overreacting when they're not
- Bullying someone then using positive re-enforcement to confuse them
- Their actions don't follow their words
- Telling someone you were only joking when you were not
- Trivializing how someone feels by saying, "You just don't understand."
- Denying whether something even happened in the first place

When you've been gaslighted for a long time, you end up feeling like you're a hollow shell of a person, you lose touch with your sense of self, you're more anxious, you question every minor thing that you do, apologize way too often than you should, and get really indecisive about minor decisions and panic about major ones.

Arguably, the most frequently used manipulative trick in the book is gaslighting, and every other manipulative technique is a variation of it. It's emotional abuse that makes a person question their very thoughts, memories, and sometimes even identities.

If you feel you are being gaslighted, it's best to talk to someone who is not directly involved in it. They will look at the situation from an unbiased position and will help you understand whether the manipulator is making you doubt your reality and perception or not.

Love Bombing

Love-bombing is when someone tries to overwhelm you with affection and extravagance – flowers every day, flattering comments, and even double and triple texts.

MANIPULATIVE PEOPLE USE this to confuse a new victim. At the start of their relationship, they may overwhelm the victim with adoration and attention so that they lower their guard and become closer and ultimately feel indebted towards the manipulator. They move too fast, too soon, and may make you feel like your boundaries are being pushed, yet you can't do much about it. In this case, you are being love-bombed. Manipulators also use this to lure in someone who's already in their circle and is about to leave.

HERE ARE some signs you're being love-bombed

- You're getting constant, overwhelming attention
- The compliments are never-ending
- The gifts are too extravagant for how well you know them
- They don't react well to you asking for space
- They may isolate you from other friends and family
- Attempting to control where you go and who you meet, all under the pretext of love
- Expecting you to reciprocate the same affection and attention they give you

Love bombing has many similarities with another manipulative tactic called 'hoovering.' Hoovering is discussed in detail in this chapter's later sections. Still, it differs from love bombing because of the time it takes place: love-bombing happens at the very beginning of a relationship, whereas hoovering occurs when the person is about to leave.

Word Salad

Have you ever been in an argument with someone, and they start throwing at you a mix of circular arguments, exaggerated claims, contradictory statements, illogical sentences?

IF YOUR ANSWER IS YES, then you have engaged in word salad.

THIS HAPPENS when you question or challenge manipulators or get a little too quick for their liking. At that point, they'll throw in a lot of projection, blaming, deflections, and denials to throw you off. They will act as if you are making a big deal out of nothing and make you doubt yourself. Though lying is second nature to them and what they do habitually, once caught, they will fervently deny all of it and cover it up with another lie.

YOU END up feeling confused and guilty – you might even take the blame they're throwing at you. And that's *precisely* what they want!

THIS TACTIC IS CONSIDERED a form of gaslighting and is one of their many tactics that helps them get out of confrontations unscathed. They leave the other person weary and frustrated, making them end the argument just for the sake of it, without reaching a solution. It is believed that narcissists tend to be the ones who engage in word salad the most.

A FEW SEMANTICS that someone engaging in a word salad might employ are circular conversations, projections and blaming, raging spirals, overgeneralizations, and sometimes just plain gibberish. Manipulators will project their own traits at you. By using phrases like, "All you do is lie and deny." Nothing will ever be their fault, and it will always be yours. No matter how senseless it may be, everything is blamed on you. In arguments with manipulators, you will just be going round and round, with no solution or consensus in sight. They will never accept their mistake and will not stop the blaming, arguments, and word salad until you put the blame on yourself.

Bread-Crumbing

Just like certain foods nourish us, certain traits nourish our relationships.

IF YOU WANT to sustain a healthy relationship, you need to put in the right mix of empathy, care, steady communication, and healthy boundaries. Those are the emotional 'nutrients' that our relationships need if we want to nourish them and keep them going.

BREAD-CRUMBING IS when you spread those emotional nutrients thin over extended periods of time; it's emotional starvation. And what happens when we get food after extended periods of starving? We gobble it up.

. . .

MANIPULATIVE PEOPLE GIVE you a big taste of their charm and charisma mixed with some love-bombing at the initial stages of your relationship. When they have you in their circle, they slowly cut off the emotional energy you were getting. If you're not aware of what's happening, you learn to be satisfied with the tiny scraps you're getting – you learn to latch onto the hope that the love-bombing that you witnessed at the start is just around the corner.

BUT IT NEVER COMES.

THUS, you become dependent on them without even realizing it. Breadcrumbing looks like a bit of affection, flattering remarks, and some gifts after months and months of neglect and emotional abuse. In your relationship with them, you might have a hard time understanding where you stand for them. One day they will be making plans with you, but the next, they flake and don't show up. Similarly, on one instance, they may be warm and affectionate, and on the next, extremely cold and distant. In the end, it leaves you confused, frustrated, and craving for their love and attention that you get in scarce amounts.

THINK HANSEL AND GRETEL – they were quite literally breadcrumbed into their doom by a witch. That's what the Dark Triad personalities do to your emotions when they breadcrumb you.

. . .

ALL OF US have manipulative tendencies and are guilty of sending a couple of flirty texts to keep someone looped in even when we had no romantic interest in them. When it's the dark triad, they'll do this intentionally and without any remorse or guilt. They do it because it makes them feel better about themselves since they are wanted by someone. They play with your emotions simply because they can, and it gives them control and power over you.

Hoovering

Have you ever had a toxic ex randomly text you, "I miss you."? Have you ever had a manipulative parent that you rarely talk to use your child to relay messages to you? Have you had a fight with your spouse, and they show up to pick you at your workplace, acting like everything is back to normal?

THAT'S the manipulator's attempt at sucking you back into the toxic relationship. This is called 'hoovering' – and sometimes it works. In fact, hoovering is the reason it takes people several tries to leave a relationship because they keep being sucked back in. This is not to be confused with sincere attempts at reconciliation; if there is a past involvement of a toxic relationship with that person, then you are likely being hovered by them.

HOOVERING AND LOVE-BOMBING might sound the same – and in a way, they are. They both use excessive gift-giving, overwhelming affection, and a lot of extravagances. The difference is that love-bombing happens just when you're about to get into a relationship with them, whereas hoovering occurs just when you're about to leave because you finally start seeing them for what they are. But both are attempts to lure you into their traps.

LOVE-BOMBING CAN LOOK like many incentives at a new workplace where you're later overburdened, scapegoated, and exploited. Whereas hoovering can look like your toxic employer raising your salary just when you've handed in your resignation letter because you finally decide you've had enough.

HOOVERING CAN KEEP people stuck in toxic dynamics for years, even decades. That's because it plays into the victim's hope that things will return to the way they used to be and that the manipulator will go back to their 'real' self, who is kinder and loves them. But that never happens. And all this extravagance is short-lived. Soon as the manipulators see that you've decided to stay, the manipulations will start again.

ONCE YOU HAVE SLIPPED AWAY, they will come right back and convince you that they have changed. They will do their best to seem as apologetic and regretful as possible, but it's all a manipulative tactic. They will shower you with extravagant gifts, declare their undying love for you, and make a number of promises to you. For example, if they didn't want to have children before, they will say that they've changed their mind, even when they probably haven't.

MANIPULATORS MAY MAKE you reminisce the past by using seemingly benign statements like, 'I'm watching our favorite movie,' or, 'I dreamt about you.' They may contact you on important dates like the holidays or your anniversary, all as a way to reminisce the good old times you had spent together in the past, perhaps during the love-bombing stage of your relationship.

THE KEY to responding to hovering behavior is to not respond at all. It helps to continue to ignore it and disengage yourself from that manipulator, such as by blocking their number and cutting them off. If you keep giving them the attention they demand from you, their actions can potentially escalate to a dangerous level, so it's best if you cut yourself out altogether earlier.

Coercive Control

Manipulators love to control and exert their power on you and on situations. Whether overtly or covertly, they will do whatever it takes to have control over your actions, thoughts, and feelings. Coercive control is an abusive tactic where the manipulator controls their victim's basic needs. This can include monitoring someone's ins and outs, controlling where and when they go, who they meet, micromanaging what they do, wear, and eat, limiting their access to family or finances, and depriving them of medical attention.

THIS IS MOTIVATED BY INSECURITIES, envy, personal gain, projection, and just the need to feel in control of someone else's life.

COERCIVE CONTROL CAN TAKE on very subtle forms. Your partner may tell you that they just want to spend more time with you, and that's why you shouldn't go out with your friends. Or a parent might control your mobility under the guise of protectiveness. More often than not, they mask their controlling behavior with love and affectionate intent. But in reality, it is all to feel a sense of control and gain benefits. Coercive control is a hostage-like situation that can look an awful lot like love, flattering, and attention, so it's tough to spot from the get-go. Identifying these subtle controlling behaviors can be difficult in the beginning, but some of the common controlling behaviors manipulators engage in include

- Being the one in control of the finances
- Isolating you from other people in your life
- They may even dictate what you wear and eat
- Cutting off your 'privileges'
- Coercing the victim to stay in the relationship because the manipulator will harm themselves or the victim

Triangulation

People with complex traits like the Dark Triad personalities aren't usually direct with their manipulations. More often than not, their manipulations are subtle and covert. Sometimes their manipulations don't even involve their victims at all.

TRIANGULATION HAPPENS when more than one person is involved in a conflict with someone manipulative. In a marital conflict where one of the spouses is manipulative, they might involve their children to take their side, ease some tension or re-enforce their superiority. However, triangulation occurs in almost any kind of relationship, including parent-child, romantic partners, and friends.

. . .

MANIPULATIVE PEOPLE INVOLVE a third person in conflicting situations to maintain a sense of control over the matter and make the actual victim feel cornered. They almost never deal in direct conversations and use a third person to relay conversations, thus creating a triangle. This technique is also used by manipulators to deflect from the original issue or to create another conflict.

THIS IS ALSO an attempt at turning a third person against their victim. A manipulative coworker who feels insecure that you got a project that they wanted to work on might go to your boss and say, "I didn't want to bring this up, but she's having relationship problems, and I did most of the work last month." Your boss is now involved in a problem that the manipulative person had with you. This could be true for other relationships as well. All of this is done to make the victim feel guilty, confused, and insecure. They might become more deeply distressed and begin doubting themselves and their reality.

THIS TRIANGULATION IS an intentional attempt by the manipulator to exert control and deflect blame from them. It keeps the victim in their trap no matter what and reinforces their superiority in the relationship.

Future Faking

Future faking is one of the most prominent and most destructive yet the most subtle tools of manipulative people and those with Dark Triad personality traits. Manipulators who engage in future faking use their victim's most intimate dreams and aspirations, string them along and eventually annihilate them.

. . .

THEY MAKE the *exact* kinds of promises that you want to hear, knowing that they'll never follow through with them. They might promise to 'someday' start a family with you, to 'someday' give you that promotion you've been asking for years, or 'someday' open up a business with you – but these promises are never delivered. Future faking is essentially comprised of over-promising and under-delivering.

FUTURE FAKING'S destruction is particularly prominent when it comes to financing. If it's an intimate partner, they'll assure you of their income potential, that they have more than enough money to support a family – and in that way, they can coax you into leaving a stable job, a city and end up putting you in a situation of coercive control. If it's your boss, they'll add extra workload and tell you it's because they're thinking of promoting you down the road. They'll hype you about how great of an opportunity it is, all the benefits and bonuses you'll be getting, and how perfect it is to your career path. Months go by, and you're still doing extra work without any of the benefits that you were promised.

FUTURE FAKING IS DONE by making empty promises of the future by the manipulator in order to satisfy their own present needs. Future faking can vary in terms of the promises made; it can be as significant as starting a family together or be something minuscule like promising to call but never following through. Either way, they are made with the intention of not fulfilling it and almost always are broken. Manipulators will begin by future faking through promises and then simultaneously use other manipulative tactics like coercive control, passive and active aggression.

. . .

You can protect yourself from future fakers by judging people by their actions instead of their words. If they've promised to build a business with you, do they have an actual plan? If they've said they're going to buy a house with you, are they saving up for it? Continue asking for updates and see if they are making too many excuses. If you see that they are just lies being covered up by excuses, it is likely future faking. Act accordingly and step out of the situation as soon as you can.

Distance yourself from a future faker as soon as possible because the consequences can be devastating. Future faking is a powerful tool because most have dreams and hopes about a certain kind of future – romantic, family-related, or professional. This manipulative tactic plays on all of those vulnerabilities and leaves us with nothing. The consequences of future faking can be emotionally and financially devastating and can leave the victims grieving for their loss over a lifetime.

Summary

Here's a summary of everything we learned in this chapter:

- There are three personalities within the Dark Triad: Narcissism, Psychopathy and Machiavellianism
- Narcissism is a personality trait that includes an inflated sense of self, grandiosity, lack of empathy and selfishness
- Psychopathy involves extreme lack of empathy, inability to experience any emotions, deceit and impulsiveness
- Machiavellian believe that it is acceptable to do whatever it takes to achieve your goals; and hence

would lie, deceive, be violent and use harmful tactics to get what they want
- These personalities employ numerous manipulative tactics, with gaslighting, love-bombing, lying, and hovering being just a few

3
NEURO-LINGUISTIC PROGRAMMING AND NON-VERBAL COMMUNICATION

Neuro-linguistic programming or NLP is a skillset that teaches you how to communicate with other people and yourself and what courses of action to take in order to achieve your desired goals. It gives practical advice on how individuals can behave, say, and express themselves to get what they want.

HEALTHY and steady communication is crucial to all relationships. It is what can make or break relationships. By communication, we don't just mean our outward expressions – we're talking about our gestures, hand movements, body language, and other non-verbal language cues as well.

A LOT OF OUR COMMUNICATION, especially non-verbal, is unconscious and reflexive. This means we interact and react without thinking about it. Our body is the first to respond, and that too, completely unconsciously. This can significantly impact our relationships – we can say and do things that make people mistrust us without even knowing about it.

NLP HELPS REGULATE THOSE UNCONSCIOUS, unwanted reflexes. It teaches us to be mindful of and to correct our internal and external monologues. This can greatly help us in influencing others and getting them to do what we want. It is a tool that can be mastered through thorough learning and practice.

THERE ARE three aspects to neuro-linguistic programming. First is the **'neuro'** aspect, which is also called 'First Access' of the neurological filtering process in NLP. This deals with the physical, mental, and emotional components of our minds. All of us have created in our heads our unique little worlds; everything in there comes from the first series of images, sounds, sensations, tastes, and smells that we've been brought up with. None of us, even if we're twins, have the same mental map. With NLP, we learn to figure the map out, scratch out the old lines and draw new ones. It helps us to dig deeper into our own selves and uncover who we are in terms of our values, beliefs, preferences, aspirations, and morals.

SECOND IS THE 'LINGUISTIC' part, also known as the 'Linguistic Map' or 'Linguistic Representation,' and it deals with how we express our mind maps to other people and ourselves. NLP teaches us to tap into the subconscious parts of our mind and notice how we interact with people and ourselves, the words we use, and the gestures we make. Observing our language can help us see our thought process better and eventually rewire and program it, which brings us to the next part.

. . .

THE THIRD IS THE 'PROGRAMMING' part which is our internal operating system which is an amalgamation of our past experiences, thoughts, and feelings, which affects the rest of our lives. NLP helps us rewire our instinctual methods of talking to people and ourselves. Once you get through the first two stages, this step comes almost naturally – if you know you're actually shaking your head while saying 'yes,' you'll be more mindful of it the next time it happens. Bringing things from the depths of your mind up to the surface is the most challenging part – the rest is a walk in the park.

MANY NLP EXPERTS say that learning NLP is like learning the language of your own mind – it's taking a deep dive into the depths of your subconscious mind, throwing out the trash thoughts, moving things around, and coming out a newer, better person. The end result makes one feel truly powerful and in control of themselves and their situations.

Non-Verbal Communication

Human beings don't just communicate with words; our entire body speaks a language of its own when we talk. In fact, our non-verbal behavior and cues make up more than half of our overall communication.

OUR FACIAL EXPRESSIONS, gestures, postures, and even tone of voice are incredibly powerful communication tools. They can be used to our advantage in social situations, whether it is at a job interview or during a date. There are so many ways that our body behaves that we are unaware of. Once we identify what they are, it can be very easy to control them and manipulate others to our advantage.

. . .

FOR EXAMPLE, our eyes twitch in confusion, lips purse in annoyance, and eyes light up with joy. We sit with our arms crossed in impersonal settings and uncross them around the people we love, we pace when we're nervous, and our legs shake in anxiety if we're sitting. Even when we're silent, we're communicating *something*.

EVERY TIME WE FEEL SOMETHING, our bodies instinctively express how we think before we can consciously form the words. You can tell that your friend likes someone by their fidgeting and nervous laughter. You can sense if someone's seething just by standing next to them. You know the anxious energy in a room by how people are pacing around or shaking their legs while sitting. You could even feel a tense air in a silent room when someone is angry, upset, or anxious.

IT'S incredible to see how our bodies can naturally react to external stimuli way before our minds do. Researchers have been studying this phenomenon for decades, and it is also where the infamous concept of the *'flight, fight or freeze'* reaction in Psychology comes from. This states that when confronted with danger, an individual's body can react in one of three ways; first, they can either flee the scene by physically running away, shouting, or screaming. Secondly, they could stay and fight the source of danger and directly confront it. Or lastly, they could freeze in their same spot until the danger goes away. Some examples to illustrate this concept can include

- Slamming the breaks when there is an animal on the road

- Encountering a vicious or angry animal while out on a walk
- Getting spooked by someone as soon as you enter a room
- Feeling uneasy when walking alone in an empty alley

In all of these scenarios, it is our body that reacts before we do. In the face of danger, physiological and hormonal changes take place within us that drive us to run, confront, or stay put. All of this is done to protect oneself.

NON-VERBAL CUES ARE fundamental communication tactics – you can use them to instill trust, comfort, and rapport or use them to cause fear, anxiety, and discomfort. Our gestures, facial expressions, the posture of our body, the length of our eye contact, our proximity to a person, and even the tone of our voice can make or break our relationships with people. We can use these non-verbal cues to build trust, draw people towards in, or we can use them to confuse people and push them away – it's our call. But what people tend to be unaware of is that despite it all, we can control each of these movements if we want to.

OUR BODY LANGUAGE is a knee-jerk reaction – we're not actively thinking about it. Sometimes, it can even give us away – you'll see people shaking their heads while saying 'yes.' So they pretend to agree with you, but really, their body is telling us that that's probably not true.

. . .

NLP TEACHES us to be more mindful of our non-verbal communication. It gives us the tools that we need to rewire our instincts so that we're able to gain people's trust instead of pushing.

The Different Kinds of Non-Verbal Communication

Facial Expression

The most common way to take cues from non-verbal communication is by looking at a person's face. A human face is a picture that can paint thousands of words in a thousand different ways. In fact, it's believed that we have over 3,000 facial expressions that are directly linked to our emotions; yet, our language consists of only 200 words to describe emotions. This tells you a lot about how important facial expressions can be to understand other individuals and to even persuade them.

WE TAKE cues from the curve of someone's lips, the wrinkling of their eyebrows, the flare of one's nostrils, the outer edges of the eyes, or the roll of their eyes. We can even identify whether a person is giving us a genuine or a fake smile. A genuine smile engages the entire face, but a fake smile only makes use of the mouth. Besides smiles, our mouths can also tell us a lot about the person. If they have tight lips and have a slight pout, it could mean that they are dissatisfied. However, if their mouth and lips are relaxed, it could mean that they are in a positive mood.

. . .

Ask Yourself: What's the person's face showing? Is the face expressive or blank? Are they reflecting interest, or do they look bored? Are they giving you a genuine smile?

Posture

Posture is absolutely essential for making a strong impression. A good posture conveys confidence, openness, strength, assurance, and a slouched one demonstrates weakness, laziness, fear, apprehension, and indifference. An open posture instills a feeling of friendliness and comfort, whereas a closed one – where your arms are crossed and you're looking to the side – will tell the person that you're disinterested and even convey hostility and anxiety. If the individual is leaning forward, it can tell you that they are actually interested in the conversation.

Ask Yourself: Is the person's body stiff, or is it relaxed and open? Are their shoulders raised? Are they leaning towards or against you? Do they seem to be comfortable around you?

Eye Contact

Eye contact indicates interest, attention and can even be used to build rapport with someone. If someone isn't meeting your eye, chances are they're uncomfortable, disinterested, or simply being rude. When they look to maintain directly at you, it can mean the opposite. They are genuinely interested in you, want to build a connection with you, and are giving you their full attention. Moreover, if a person does not maintain eye contact with you for very long and keeps looking away, it could be an indicator of deceit.

. . .

OUR PUPILS CAN ALSO BE cues to identify an individual's behavior with you. Dilated pupils can mean that they will respond favorably to you. A person's blinking rate will also be an indicator of their interest and attention; for example, if they blink frequently and a lot, they are stressed and potentially lying.

ASK YOURSELF: Is the person meeting your eye? How long is the duration of the eye contact? Are they blinking too much or too little? Are their pupils dilated?

Tone of Voice

The tone in which you say something matters – this includes the timing of your sentences, the volume of your voice, the emphasis on certain words, the pace of your speech, and any underlying sarcasm, anger, or inflection in your voice. Your tone of voice can give away your intentions and motives.

A LOW VOICE exhibits confidence and power; it's even considered to be attractive. Alternatively, people who spoke with a higher frequency are viewed by others as gentle and benevolent. Sometimes, high-frequency voices are also associated with fear and nervousness.

IF SPEAKING IN A MONOTONE VOICE, it may appear that the individual is bored or uninterested. Controlling your vocal tone does require a lot of practice, compared to the other non-verbal communication cues. But once mastered, it can have a considerable influence on others. That is why individuals of the Dark Triad are likely to use this cue to their benefit. For example, psychopaths tend to carry a monotonous and low vocal tone that makes them appear uninterested and intimidating to others. Therefore, a manipulator might alter their tone depending on what they need out of a situation.

Ask Yourself: Are they being sarcastic? Does the person's voice exhibit confidence or warmth? Do they sound interested? Do they seem to speak in a monotonous, high-pitched, or low-pitched tone?

Proximity

People are generally very protective of their personal space – and it's entirely natural to be. Proximity refers to the physical distance between individuals.

It tells you a lot about the closeness and type of relationship two people have. For example, if you were to randomly walk into a café and look around, you'd be able to tell whether someone's sitting with their partner, their family, their friends, or their coworkers, just by looking at the distance between them.

Proximity can determine how favorably one views the other; that is, the closer they are, the more favorably they see you. Similarly, if someone appears to be physically distant or pulling away, it means they are likely not interested in maintaining a connection. We keep strangers far apart, friends and family closer, and intimate partners the closest. The physical distance between other people and us is a reflection of our emotional space from them. The closer we are to them, the more comfortable and intimate we are likely to be with them.

However, keep in mind that this may vary depending on different cultures. Forsome, proximity is not directly proportional to affinity. For example, people in Latin America tend to stand more closely when communicating, yet anyone from North America might find that amount of distance too close for comfort.

A PERSON, not your friends and family, crossing the socially acceptable 18 inches of distance from you might make you uncomfortable. This is likely what manipulators do and take advantage of as well.

ASK YOURSELF: Is a person getting too close for comfort? How do they react if I express my discomfort? What are they gaining by establishing my trust?

Hand Gestures

Some people talk with their hands – their gestures are all over the place, they're excitable and enthusiastic, they drum their hands, tap their thighs, and touch their faces. Some other easily noticeable and controllable hand gestures include using fingers to depict numerical values, waving, and pointing.

HAND GESTURES CAN REFLECT someone's anxieties and excitement. Usually, manipulators are very calm and collected and don't engage in a lot of hand gestures.

MOREOVER, hand gestures can vary depending on different cultures. That is, some cultures depict hand gestures, such as a peace sign, differently. Some of the most common gestures people engage in include:

- A clenched fist when angry, irritated, or nervous
- A thumbs up or thumbs down to show approval or disapproval
- A V-Sign to show peace or victory

Hand gestures and movements can signal certain emotions and thoughts a person is experiencing, thus paying close attention to them is important. For example, if someone is putting their hands in their pockets, it could mean that they are lying, hiding something, or just nervous. Moreover, when communicating, individuals are more likely to point at someone they share the most affinity with.

ADDITIONALLY, if someone is supporting their head with one head while listening to you, it means that they are trying to focus and listen intently. However, if they support their head with two hands, it likely reflects boredom and lack of interest.

BY WATCHING out for these cues, you can influence other individuals by showing your approval, interest, and feelings. It can thus foster feelings of trust in them as well.

ASK YOURSELF: Does the person appear to be bored or uninterested based on the positioning of their arms? Are they using a lot of hand gestures? Are they hiding their hands in their pockets?

Arms and Legs

Another useful nonverbal communication cue to look out for and control is the positioning of arms and legs. Sometimes, people consciously control their facial expressions in social situations. That is why they transfer most of their nonverbal expression towards their arms and legs, hence making them excellent tools for insight.

OUR ARMS CAN BE the gateway to our feelings and emotions. For example, open arms, such as by putting them behind one's neck, can indicate openness, comfort, confidence, and just laid-back and relaxed behavior in general. On the other hand, if the arms are crossed, it could mean that the person is closed off, angry, anxious, vulnerable, or just generally have a closed mind.

CLASPING one's hands behind their back can also mean that they are bored, anxious, or even angry. Moreover, rapidly tapping fingers or fidgeting one's hands can mean that they are in a tense state of mind or bored, frustrated, or anxious. Moreover, when someone places their hands on their hips, it can be a way of ensuring and exerting dominance and control. It can also be a sign of potential aggressiveness. Hence, manipulators tend to use this nonverbal communication cue most often.

WHEN IT COMES to the positioning of legs, look out for whether they too are crossed or open. Crossed legs may mean that the individual is nervous, reserved, and in need of privacy. Contrastingly, if they are open, they may indicate openness and relaxation. The direction of the legs can also tell a lot about a person; for example, the person they are pointing towards is likely to be someone they are most comfortable with and have the most affection for. Hence, if they are pointing away from someone, they may indicate feelings of hostility and dislike.

ASK YOURSELF: Are the person's arms crossed or open? Are they being closed off, anxious, nervous, or angry? Where are their legs pointing towards? Are their legs crossed or open?

The Body Language of Manipulators

Manipulators are everywhere. If you have doubts about someone constantly manipulating you, there are nonverbal cues you can look out for. Besides verbal communication, a manipulator may use nonverbal methods to influence individuals. Their body language can be subtle, persuasive, charming. Other times, their language can be threatening, overpowering, and daunting. Sometimes manipulators get what they want by flattery, and other times it's by violation – body language differs in both cases. Manipulators use deceptive body language to coerce and control individuals to gain their own benefit. Thankfully, there are ways of spotting a manipulator based on how their body acts and reacts to different situations.

ADDITIONALLY, when it comes to certain personality types like narcissists or psychopaths, the body language is generally very obviously hostile – it's in their predatory gazes, their too-close-for-comfort bodies, and entirely disinterested and downright bored demeanor.

. . .

There's no one-size-fits-all approach in understanding the tactics that manipulative people might use to get what they want, but a few of them are the most common. You can look out for these tactics when observing them.

They Violate Your Personal Space

As mentioned in the previous section, the physical distance we maintain between ourselves and other people reflects our emotional distance and comfort with them.

A person, not your friends and family, crossing the socially acceptable 18 inches of distance can do two things: make you uncomfortable or trick your brain into thinking that the person is safe. Manipulators make use of the latter to gain your trust and eventually control you. They might cross the comfortable distance too soon; they will put a hand on your back, lean in too close even after you've stepped back to readjust, repeatedly touch your arm and shoulder. This is them trying to use body language tricks to their advantage – don't fall for it. It's their way of establishing dominance, and getting too close too soon.

This is the manipulator trying to create a false sense of intimacy and trust. They want to form a 'bond' or closeness with you, despite you stepping away and showing obvious discomfort. They'll continue doing this even if you make your boundaries clear to them – persistence is how they get away with manipulating people for so long.

They 'Mirror' You

This is a very common tactic manipulators use subtly to influence and control you without you realizing it. Mirroring refers to when someone absorbs everything that you say and do and reflect it back to you during your interactions.

MIRRORING IS A PREVALENT MANIPULATION TACTIC, especially with same-sex friendships. People who mirror you will start liking the same clothes that you like, take on your tone of voice, hairstyle, favorite song is suddenly their favorite as well – that's the extreme example, but it happens subtly. They can go so far as even mimicking your breathing!

WE ALL KNOW someone who changes their opinion as soon as someone disagrees with them. They observe your 'baseline' movements and behaviors, and begin to mimic it in situations.

A LOT OF THE TIME, people who do this have a distorted self-perception. Many other times, they're trying to get into your good books just enough to use you and sabotage your life. They want to build rapport with you and have a closer relationship, and they believe that they will get this through behaving and reacting as you do.

MIRRORING IS A GREAT TRUST-BUILDING TACTIC, and it is only malicious in the hands of manipulative people. You can tell if someone is mirroring you to a toxic extent if you observe them in a different group of people. If they're acting like a whole other person with them, be warned. Alternatively, when you confront them about it, and they shift their behavior, become too defensive, or immediately change their behavior, then they are likely mirroring you.

They Blink Unusually

An individual's gaze and the blinking rate is a useful way of identifying their internal state. If someone is blinking too much or too little, be careful. Blinking rapidly is a sign of stress and dishonesty, deceit, fear, or discomfort.

ON THE OTHER HAND, blinking too little is downright creepy and is known to be a tell-tale sign of psychopathy. Psychopaths have a notorious 'predatory stare' where they fixate their gaze on their victim to get a sense of gratification and power. No one likes being stared at intensely for more than a couple of seconds, and manipulators take advantage of the discomfort caused in the wake of their predatory gaze. For them, it is a way to establish their dominance on the victim, trick them into believing that they are the ones in control.

BLINKING SLOWLY IS ALSO a sign of deceit and lying. If an individual is lying to you, they might blink less or not at all. Once they are back to normal conversation and not lying, their blinking may increase and return to a normal rate. It's important to observe and identify what the baseline blinking rate is of manipulators, which will then help you to assess when blinking becomes rapid or slows down.

They Self-Sooth

When the manipulator is a no-shame psychopath, they might self-soothe as a way to signal to you that they're nervous – they're not; it's just a party trick they use to induce sympathy or guilt. Individuals in the Dark Triad not only desperately seek control, but they also often engage in tactics that will help them gain sympathy from their victims. They may perform self-soothing acts to depict their anxiety and nervousness, though they may be feeling none of those things; it's just their way of deceiving their victims.

SOMETIMES, the manipulator unconsciously feels guilty for what they know they're about to do. In that case, you'll see them trying to soothe themselves by rubbing their necks, shifting their weight on their feet, stroking their own arms, tapping their feet, or scratching their chins. This is them simply trying to alleviate their own guilt because of their manipulations.

SCRATCHING their chin is a way to show their victim that they have low confidence and are in need of their validation and support. In fact, it is a manipulative tactic to get their victims to do favors for them and basically get them to do what they want, even if they are perfectly capable of doing it themselves.

IF YOU THINK someone is a manipulator, especially if you suspect their personality is one of the three dark triads, then realize that you're probably being manipulated subtly – and step away. Another way of identifying whether their behaviors are self-soothing, is to again identify what their baseline behaviors are and compare whether the self-soothing acts are a natural part of their identity or just a ruse.

They Express Empathy That Isn't There

Manipulators don't have empathy –that's quite literally how they manipulate so well for so long. The rest of us feel it when someone is hurt, and the guilt is so uncomfortable that we either stop what we're doing or amend our ways. The defining trait of individuals in the Dark Triad is their profound lack of empathy. But this is not to be confused with the fact that they cannot recognize other individual's emotions and feelings. They very well can; after all, that is how they maneuver their actions to control their victims. However, they don't feel or experience these emotions. They can only identify them on a cognitive level, but not on an emotional one. The only exception when these Dark Triad personalities would experience emotions is when they are frustrated, angry, or upset.

MANIPULATORS ARE aware that humans long for connection. They use this fact to their advantage by faking empathy and building a connection so they can later influence the individual. In the initial stages of their relationship with their victims, manipulators will identify their victim's emotions, such as whether they are showing genuine positive feelings for them or not, and then use this information to take advantage of others.

MANIPULATORS LIKE PSYCHOPATHS are either biologically unable to be empathetic or, like narcissistic, they have really shallow empathy that they use to serve their own purposes. Narcissistic or Machiavellian can usually tell what the other person is feeling; they spend a lot of time studying people, figuring out their vulnerabilities, and knowing what makes them tick. This means they *do* have a basic understanding of what makes the other person feel a certain way –the problem is that narcissists and Machiavellian weaponize them against everyone. They don't feel any remorse for these acts or identify anything wrong with such behaviors.

PSYCHOPATHS, on the other hand, barely even recognize normal human emotions like compassion, pain, or grief; these emotions are unknown territories to them in other people because they've barely felt those themselves. In some ways, they were born with a lack of empathy and had never truly felt any of these emotions to be able to identify or understand them. Similarly, Machiavellians and Narcissists only use empathy as tools to help control others and meet their ends. They may experience certain emotions, but they do not see it as anything that influences their actions or make them feel bad.

WHEN MANIPULATORS EXPRESS ANY EMPATHY, like putting a hand on your shoulder when you're sad or telling you they're sorry they hurt you, it's usually very superficial. It feels empty, and there's a high chance that their apologies are simply one of the many tools they use to keep slithering back into your life.

They're Too Much of an Open Book

It's okay to be vulnerable or reveal specific details about yourself to certain people – but if someone you just met is telling you their life story already, tread with caution. Much like love-bombing, where they overwhelm you with gifts and affection, manipulators can also overwhelm you with too much of their information. Narcissists, in particular, will go on and on about themselves. Manipulators, on the whole, tend to share their problems, difficulties, and life story in hopes of gaining your sympathy and rope you into their manipulative tactics. Chances are, all of these narratives are probably not even true and just a ruse to lure you in.

MANIPULATIVE PEOPLE REVEAL TOO MUCH TOO SOON, creating a false sense of familiarity that they, later on, use to get what they want. In their attempt to create a stronger bond with you, they will share details about themselves, compelling and even expecting you to do the same. They want you to see them as honest, reliable, and trustworthy people – but they're not any of those things. This strategic tactic is very well thought out by manipulators, who may fabricate stories where they appear to be heroic and honest. Since they are master liars, it isn't much of a problem for them to weave together elaborate false stories.

THEREFORE, it's possible that the story they're narrating isn't even true – they're just excellent storytellers and trick you into their carefully spun web of lies. Tread with caution around manipulators, and be wary of everything they tell you.

They Conceal Their Emotions

There's something called an *emblematic slip* –these are the slips that happen without the person realizing it. When someone is concealing an emotion or lying, these deceitful feelings come out one way or the other through our nonverbal communication cues- and these are termed as emblematic slips. We can illustrate this with the same example we gave before: saying an audible '*Yes*' but shaking your head. When people do this, they actually want to say no, but some form of guilt or responsibility is making them say yes. People usually make these gestures without knowing it.

THIS THEORY of unintentional slips was presented by Darwin, who posed that these gestures were innate – a light shrug of the shoulder, or rotation of your hand, or the tone of your voice can indicate deception. These slips give us information about what the person *actually* wants – and manipulative people engage in many of these emblematic slips. They may be masters at lying, but they're often involuntary movements they don't notice or control.

MANIPULATORS TEND TO conceal their hidden aggression with their victims, especially during the start of their relationship. In order to build closer attention with their prospective victim, the manipulators try to hide their true aggressive intentions towards them so as to appear affectionate and charming. This is when emblematic slips come out, as they are unaware of controlling these movements.

They Weaponize Your Guilt

Manipulators are masterminds at evading responsibility –and to dodge anything at all, it needs to be redirected. When something goes wrong, manipulators will be found throwing blame left, right and center. They will never own up to a mistake or take responsibility for any issues, even when they know that they are at fault. This is another manipulative tactic that they use to control their victims and exert dominance.

. . .

GUILT IS A VERY HUMAN EMOTION – all of us feel it. If we didn't, we'd quite literally be murderous psychopaths. Most of us feel guilt when we do something wrong, and it is such an uncomfortable feeling that we're quick to make amends. That is why it is one of the most powerful tactics used by manipulators.

MANIPULATORS, on the other hand, don't take responsibility for anything. That's primarily because they're too egotistical, but, more importantly, they're unable to sit with *any* uncomfortable feeling: grief, anger, regret, and even boredom. A manipulator's natural inclination is to throw any uncomfortable feeling outward instead of sitting with them.

THEY DO the same with guilt as well.

WHENEVER SOMETHING GOES WRONG, and they're involved even in the *slightest*, they're quick to blame other people. For those who *aren't* manipulative, we're likely to take on an added guilt and fix the situation to avoid the discomfort. That is why manipulators try to guilt-trip their victims whenever they get the chance. They make their unhappiness clear to you, making you feel like you are responsible for fixing the problem and uplifting their mood. And this tactic is quite effective because if they have made you guilty for the way they are feeling, you are likely going to do whatever it takes to fix the problem. This is especially effective for victims who tend to be more compassionate.

MANIPULATORS WILL MAKE you believe that you are the bad guy and they are the constant victims, or that each problem in their relationship stems from the victims' lack of concern for the manipulator. For example, they may use phrases like, "If you cared about me, you wouldn't..."

THAT WAY, the manipulators get away with not just throwing the blame onto other people but also evading responsibility. This is how they weaponize a very natural, human reaction like guilt to their benefit.

- Some of the telltale signs of someone guilt-tripping you includes
- Make passive-aggressive remarks
- Deny they are irritated, even though their actions show otherwise
- Use nonverbal cues to show their dissatisfaction; for example, sighing, shrugging, or crossing their arms
- Make no effort to fix the situation or problem themselves

They Appeal to Your Morality

If you tell them lying is amoral in your world, suddenly they'll share a story about how they're so honest that it gets them into nasty situations. There's a particular brand of narcissists called communal narcissists who use spirituality and religion as tactics of manipulation. A considerable amount of religious and cult leaders have been noted to be manipulators simply because of this effective tactic. According to the research, amongst a manipulator's top few favorite positions of power is a priest. Very few people dare to question priests, rabbis, or imams – or any other religion's authority that you might subscribe to.

. . .

MANIPULATIVE PEOPLE THRIVE to be in that position, where no one can question them, where every word they utter is revered, and every action is celebrated. They are truly admired, feeding their egos. And they can influence individuals for their own benefit in the name of morality. Positions of religious leaders are thus the favorite positions for individuals in the Dark Triad. These individuals take advantage of moral emotions in individuals to serve their own benefits.

THIS IS an effective tactic to use to manipulate others because we all have an innate need to help society and work for the common good. This fact makes individuals vulnerable to following the authority of religious and moral leaders.

AND EVEN ON the off-chance that someone *does* end up questioning this manipulative person in such an exalted position, people around them would automatically raise a questioning brow on the skeptical person instead. That person will be seen as the malicious one who is attempting to take advantage, rather than the manipulator themselves.

IT'S a real catch-22 that manipulative people *absolutely* thrive in. Who wants to violate their own value system and disrespect the priest?

They Twist Everyone's Realities

One of the most effective tricks that manipulators use is twisting people's realities. They'll do this by gaslighting and lying to people, and you'll often hear a lot of these from a manipulator:

- "That never happened."
- "I think you're being a little too sensitive."
- "It was just a joke. Relax."
- "Are you sure all of this happened?"

They may even engage in physically gaslighting people – like moving objects and then denying that they did so. Or going to a social gathering but saying they were never there. All of this makes the victim doubt their own perception, feelings, and thoughts. They may begin to question everything around them and start mistrusting their own selves. As a result, their realities become distorted, and they eventually become dependent on the manipulator.

EVERYONE'S REALITIES ARE DIFFERENT, and we all have our own unique ways of making sense of the world. That's how we feel grounded. To have someone question how you feel makes you doubt yourself too. Soon, you'll start second-guessing, double-checking, self-doubting every move that you make and every word you say. This may also keep you on edge and paranoid at all times. It creates a pattern of feeling and thoughts that become embedded inside you, which makes it hard to let go of even when the manipulator has long been cut off from your life.

THE MANIPULATORS not only make you question your own sanity but make other people question your authenticity as well. They can involve a third person in your situation who may take their side, ultimately leaving you isolated and cornered. This tactic can truly be crazy-making and leave the victim even insane.

. . .

BUT WHAT DOES THAT ACCOMPLISH? Well, if it comes down to it, people –including yourself –will be less likely to believe you. They'll take the manipulator's word over yours. This tactic often happens subtly, and manipulators use it to build their own credibility by diminishing other people's. It makes them increase their dominance and control over their victims. It also allows their victims to become more dependent on the manipulator since they can no longer trust their own words.

THEY TWIST everyone's realities and create their own – they'll make everyone think that *their* version of the truth is the only correct version out there. Manipulators are masterminds at creating doubts in safe places, reframing people's worlds to their own liking, and bending realities to their whims. And since they can lie and deceive without much effort, this tactic becomes even easier for them to use and take advantage of their victims.

They're Always the Victims

Manipulators fabricate facts and exaggerate situations in which they're victims. Manipulators play the victim card whenever someone questions or criticizes the manipulator's behavior. This helps them justify abuse, seek attention, and evade responsibility. Manipulative behavior is like second nature for individuals with Dark Triad personality traits, especially narcissists.

WHEN SOMEONE PLAYS the 'woe is me' card, they're more likely to gain someone else's sympathy, have more people on their side, and control everyone's narrative. It also distracts people from the manipulator's behavior, who is no longer the aggressor but a victim who probably caused the problem and instigated aggression. In fact, it is a way of controlling other individuals and make them do what they want.

SOME OF THE ways manipulators become the 'victims' in situations can be through exaggerating their mental or health problems they have, playing the martyr or the weak individual in an argument, and exaggerating a shortcoming in their lives.

PEOPLE WHO ARE extra-sensitive by nature are more likely to fall prey to this because it's harder for them to detach from other people's emotions. Compassionate individuals, who hear other individual's problems and wish to care and fix them, might particularly be easy targets for manipulators. Empathetic people are usually groomed by abusers to enable and assist them in their quest for power; this is known as proxy abuse. Moreover, individuals who are good-natured, conscientious, have a sense of duty, and have a protective or nurturing instinct, are more likely to fall victim to this particular tactic by manipulators.

IF YOU SEE someone who constantly is the victim in every narrative they tell you or situation they are in with you, it is likely that they may be manipulating you. Step back and identify the facts before moving forward.

Their Actions Are Exaggerated

To understand exaggerated expressions and actions, you need to know what the norm is. We all know the standard speech, tone, body positioning, verbal cues, and eye movements that are considered 'normal.' We know when the flirting is getting too much, the gifts are excessive, the aggression is disproportionate, and the competitiveness is toxic. If someone is smiling way too widely, you know it's deceptive.

MANIPULATORS EXAGGERATE their expressions to give an air of intensity to their typically shallow emotions. When it comes to manipulators, every word and action will feel out-of-the-norm. They're trying to manipulate you and throw you off. Manipulators also engage in a lot of hyperbole. With them, things aren't just bad; they're terribly awful. The love-bombing is a part of the exaggerated expressions; people generally don't go all-in with the gift-giving unless they're trying to win you over. With manipulators, they will go above and beyond by gifting you extravagant things, making promises for the future, declaring their undying love to you, and many more exaggerated actions – all too soon. These actions, however, continue throughout the course of the relationship even when it has matured, and perhaps the love has died. The exaggerated actions could even be seen from their aggression. Not only that but in hopes to gain sympathy from the victim, they would also exaggerate their circumstances and feelings. For example, they would tell them, "No one has ever loved me before."

MUCH LIKE LYING, exaggerating, too, is an art mastered by manipulators. All of this is done by them to exert a certain sense of dominance over their victims and create an imbalance of power in their relationship. This tactic is especially used by narcissists most commonly because they have an exaggerated sense of self, believing themselves to be the absolute best and superior to everyone. They will exaggerate their talents and accomplishments to the point that it would all be a lie. All of these manipulative tactics, more often than not, work effectively because most people are not able to see through their charades.

You Feel it In Your Gut

If we were to trust our gut feelings more often, we'd all get ourselves out of tricky situations very early on. Your gut knows the predatory looks, the love-bombing, the subtle manipulations, and the reality-altering tactics *way* before your conscious mind does. You'll feel the unease around them. You'll notice how your energy depletes when they're in your vicinity. You will feel emotionally drained in a social setting that's suddenly all about them. Most of the time, we don't trust our gut feelings because the facts are missing; however, when we take a step back to notice the repeated subtle and harmful behaviors directed towards us, it might be worthwhile to acknowledge these gut feelings. Our gut feeling knows more than we perceive it to; it notices all the covert ways that manipulators use to maneuver our behavior, influence our decisions, and make us feel bad overall.

IN A LOT OF CASES, our gut and intuition are right. If there is something we feel is wrong or off, there is probably a reason why we are. Noticing the red flags early on, and acknowledging the feelings you might be getting in your gut, might save you from further manipulative tactics employed by Dark Trait personalities. These tactics they use initially with you might just be the tip of the iceberg, and there is a lot more they might be hiding up their sleeves. Talk to the person when you notice alarming signs, even if they may not be as upsetting. If it's happened once, it might very well be a misunderstanding, but if it's happening several times, don't let it slip. Acknowledge the problem and hold them accountable.

THEREFORE, trust your gut the first time it tries to tell you something isn't right, and run for the hills.

Summary

Here's a summary of everything we learned in this chapter:

- NLP is a technique used to teach individuals the different ways they can behave in order to achieve their goals
- It focuses on nonverbal communication cues such as body language, facial expression, eye contact, gestures, and more
- We also take a look at the nonverbal communication tactics employed by manipulators and Dark Triad personalities

4
DARK PSYCHOLOGY OF PERSUASION

To influence people is a superpower; it's a skill that needs to be shaped, honed, and mastered before you use it. The good thing is, the art of persuasion has been backed with immense amounts of research, and we'll be giving you a rundown of the science behind persuasion and how to use it to get people to do what you want.

THIS IS the part where we tell you that manipulation and persuasion are two different things.

PERSUASION IS A COMMUNICATION TACTIC; there's nothing fundamentally wrong with it. It basically means using tactics to influence other people so that they perform actions that would benefit them and the persuader. It offers the advantages one might receive after performing the action the persuader wants them to do; in a lot of ways, it is quite like a business deal.

. . .

OUR EVERYDAY LIFE is filled with people trying to persuade us: from service providers and salespeople to our close-knit friends and family. Companies want their product to be the best in the market, and for that, they have to reach a sales quota, for which they have to *persuade* the buyers. Politicians need to *persuade* people to vote for them. Lawyers need to persuade the judge or jury to make a decision in their favor, and so on. In our lives, it is safe to say that we are being persuaded in ways that are also so subtle that we don't even notice we are being persuaded. For example, advertisements display tempting images of food that make us want to go and buy them, to taste them for ourselves. The marketing industry constantly uses clever tactics to overtly or covertly persuade people to buy certain products or services.

WANTING people to be on our side is a very human thing and at the core of socializing with one another. It's not inherently harmful; just damaging when certain personality types use it to get what they want. Only then it turns into a nefarious tool for coercion and maligning others. Convincing someone to buy something by offering them incentives is different than manipulation: manipulation means the person's choice is removed. Therefore, persuasion is much more ethical to use than manipulation if you want to get people to do what you want. Of course, the choice lies with the people if they want to perform the action or not, but for the most part, it is neither dehumanizing nor as harmful as manipulation.

PERSUASION IS DONE BY FACTS, experiences, stories, and knowledge, whereas manipulation is more subtle and committed with malicious intent in mind. In persuasion, all facts are provided to the individual, and every bit of information is brought to their attention. The intent behind the convincing and persuasion is also obvious, which isn't the case with manipulation. The motive behind the tactic is the difference between persuasion and manipulation. People who rely on Dark Psychology as a means to persuade never want someone to change their minds and tend to get hostile when they do, whereas when you're simply persuading someone, you're generally okay with however they react and don't take it personally. This is because usually, persuasion is not done exclusively for the gain of the persuader. Manipulation is simply done by a manipulator to reach an end goal, satisfy their needs, or make themselves feel better.

However, what's common between both tools is the existence of influence. The manipulator or persuader both tend to be individuals who are either in an influential position or have qualities that make them influential. Therefore, it can be said that not everyone can be a master manipulator or persuader. It requires practice, power, natural qualities of charisma, and more. We will be going into more detail about the differentiating factors between persuasion and manipulation in the upcoming sections.

Persuasion Techniques

Persuasion isn't something that only marketers and salesmen use; you can use these techniques too. Learning these tactics will enable you to negotiate better and get people to do what you want, whether it's in a professional or social setting. Of course, it won't be like manipulation where the person will somehow be forced to do what you want, but it will nonetheless have a considerable influence on their decision-making.

. . .

PERSUASION TECHNIQUES HAVE BEEN STUDIED for ages, and in the late 20th century, psychologists found out that **NLP is the basis of most persuasive techniques.** A lot of these techniques are based on empathy and understanding. Other methods include reward, punishment, positive and negative re-enforcement, but those lean more towards the manipulative territory when used against other adults, and the line between ethical and non-ethical often becomes blurred in these cases. That's one of the significant differences between persuasion and dark psychology.

EMPATHY-BASED persuasive techniques require you to understand the person you're trying to persuade and empathize with their visual, auditory, cognitive, and emotional stimulations. This will help you put yourself in another person's shoes and see what they're most likely to be persuaded by. It gives you insight into what would likely be something that might convince them. For example, for some people, providing them with the facts in a rational manner would be a stronger persuading factor. However, for others, they might be convinced if you tug at their emotions and appeal to their emotional side. Understanding the individual you want to persuade and looking at their prospective stimulations is an effective tactic that can go a long way.

THE KIND of persuasion tactics you need depends on the nature of the person you're dealing with. To understand that, pay close attention to how they talk and how their mind responds. If they're saying, "I see." they're visual learners. If they're saying, "I hear what you are saying," they're more likely to be persuaded by the audio stimulus. On the other hand, "I feel that" are more likely to be swayed by emotions. It's believed that females are likely to respond to emotional appeals, however, that is not true for all. Contrastingly, auditory and visual appeals tend to be more effective with males.

ANOTHER PERSUASION TECHNIQUE you can use is the **mirror-based approach.** This tactic works on the fact that we tend to like and be more agreeable towards those people who are like us. If you match the body language, posture, language, and other subtle gestures of the person in front of you, they'll instinctively warm up to you. This is a compelling technique, even if it seems a bit awkward at first. We don't mean that you outright copy each of their movements, but to do it in a subtle manner with specific covert actions. For example, watch out for the kind of language they use, the certain words they frequently incorporate in their speech, their tone, voice, speed, and pitch, and then respond in a similar manner. Another subtle yet extremely effective technique to influence others is to mirror their posture and pose. When you engage with a person on their level, you're more effectively able to build trust and rapport with them and get them to do what you want.

CREATING **a need** is another tactic of persuasion that works wonders. You can use people's fundamental needs for a home, for loving people, self-actualization, and self-esteem to get them to do what you like. Marketers use this tactic all the time to sell their items – they'll tell you that buying their products will make you and your loved ones feel safe, respected, and loved. This creates a need that previously the buyers were unaware of, and they're more inclined to fill that gap up by buying the products being marketed to them. Moreover, they might also start a pitch by asking potential customers if they have noticed the absence of a certain product or a need unfulfilled. They may even exaggerate to a certain degree, making it sound like the need must be fulfilled immediately, for example, that of protection and security. They'll highlight the rising rate of theft and break-ins in the customer's neighborhood, which would allow them to feel unsafe. Then, the marketer or salesperson will jump in to pitch the safety alarm product that would solve this problem by protecting their home. It's all an elaborate and subtle game that is highly effective for most individuals.

SIMILARLY, appealing to social needs is a similar and effective method that people apply to persuade one another. Somewhere deep inside of us is the need to be popular and to gain prestige – studies have shown that people are more likely to purchase products that promise a higher status or whose marketing plays into our primal need to be well-respected. This is what most makeup brands tend to do. They take advantage of female's need for validation in terms of how she looks, and design their marketing campaigns and sales pitch around that. For example, these would likely include slogans that talk about how women would look instantly beautiful and attractive by using their products or services.

ANOTHER EFFECTIVE APPROACH that people tend to comply with is when you get one person to agree to a small request and follow that up with a much larger request; the second one is what you *actually* want from them. Individuals are more likely to comply with a bigger and more significant request later on if they initially comply with a smaller one. Had they been asked directly to make the bigger request, they would not have complied; but through this approach, their likelihood to comply increases.

. . .

WHILE MASTERING the approaches we just mentioned is usually enough of a skillset to help you persuade people, there are more bonus techniques that you can make use of as well if you want to go the extra mile. This is called the **foot in the door** technique; for example, your friend asking for help with assignments once or twice sets precedence for every time after. By getting you to agree to a small favor, your friend effectively puts a foot to your door and leaves an entrance open for bigger favors. Somehow, you are likely to feel the need to honor your friend, which drives you to agree to the bigger favor. Not only that, but another reason for compliance is the need to act consistently with previous behaviors. If you have previously agreed to the first favor, your need to act consistently will drive you to agree to the subsequent one.

MANY DOOR-TO-DOOR SALESPEOPLE tend to use this approach to sell their products and services. For example, if a salesperson stands outside the store persuading individuals to buy a small bar of chocolate and succeeds at it, they will be more likely to convince the same people to enter the store to browse more variety of chocolates.

THE OPPOSITE to this is the **go big and then small** persuasive tactic where you'd start off by making an unrealistic request and follow it up with a smaller and more realistic one that you *actually* need the other person to do. This makes the person feel as if the second request is reasonable because it's placed relative to a highly unreasonable one, and the person is more likely to be persuaded this way. This comparison between the two favors drives the individuals to believe the other one is easier to do and so are more likely to agree to it. An easy example to illustrate this tactic is if you ask your friend if they could borrow $100, when they obviously deny, you then ask them if at least borrowing $20 would be possible. There's a pretty good chance that they would agree to this smaller request. The aim of this technique is to first ask for something which the person would obviously say no to and then move on to the actual request. These people would not say no to you twice or find the second request simpler, and overall just feel like they have to owe the other person for denying their request. This is a very effective persuasive tactic that can lead to compliance, especially if the two requests you make are similar.

SIMILAR TO THIS is an **anchor bias** – if you've ever bargained in the flea market, you'll know what we're talking about. This is the first offer that you make to the seller, also called the anchor price, and it sets the tone for further negotiations. If your initial price is meager, you'll get off with a good bargain after the negotiations with the seller have ended. Let's say you want to buy a vase that the buyer has set to $20. Your anchor price should be somewhere between $5 to $8 – and then you'll go back and forth with the seller before coming to a price of $12 to $15. Had you started off with $10, you'd have negotiated a price of perhaps $18. This is a powerful persuasion tactic when it comes to pricing because it lowers your anchor point; hence, you would have a better chance of persuading people to do what you need.

PEOPLE ALSO MAKE use of the power of **reciprocity** to persuade others – scratch someone's back, and they'll scratch yours. This is almost a social obligation; if someone does a favor for you, then you're more inclined to do one for them out of mutual respect and reciprocity. Businesses also utilize this tactic by offering 'extra's and 'discounts' – they'll provide the same items they usually do but at a reduced price, which compels people to purchase their products. Moreover, after purchasing a product, when companies ask you to sign up for their newsletter and give them your email address, out of kindness, you are likely going to provide it to them. Human beings value equality, and we don't like to feel like we owe other people –it's a very uncomfortable feeling to sit with. We naturally do not feel good about being indebted to someone for very long, so when the opportunity to repay the debt comes along, we are more likely to return the favor regardless of what the nature of the favor is.

USE this desire to balance things out to your advantage and influence the behaviors of others. A good approach to reciprocity would be to commit small acts of unconditional kindness, and people will do what you ask them out of mutual affection. People do this in the professional realms of their world all the time: they do favors for strangers, they help one another, they raise public slogans, and they build up organizations. All of this simply by helping one another. Of course, don't be too over the top and steer this into the love-bombing, gift-giving territory – *that* would be manipulation. Reciprocate in moderation!

ANOTHER PERSUASION TACTIC that most people love to use is showing yourself to be the **authority**. Psychology has long uncovered how individuals can naturally be so easily influenced by those in positions of authority. So much so that they would cause harm to someone else if a credible authority asks them to do it. Therefore, appearing authoritative can go a long way in persuading individuals and getting them to do what you want. You can appear authoritative by displaying your credibility and knowledge in the relevant field. Moreover, you could also increase your persuasiveness by having authority figures endorse your pitch or advertisements; for example, by asking your business' CEO to endorse a knowledgeable person or a celebrity. By displaying your education and credentials, you are also likely to increase your influence on others. For example, individuals would be more likely to follow the advice of their doctor if the doctors' degree is displayed on the wall.

MOREOVER, we also discussed earlier how finding mutual interests and similarities could help you increase your influence on other people and get them to do what you want. This technique can also come useful in **bringing someone on your side and creating unity**. You can form this unity by identifying if you belong to the same group, have a shared identity, have an obvious similarity that not many people share, or have similar goals. This will bring them on your side and will likely allow them to listen and give you a chance. This tactic is most often used by politicians who also create a sense of unity amongst the voters by focusing on the community values and shared similarities. We will be discussing this in further detail in the upcoming sections, but let's give you an example to understand this tactic better. Barrack Obama, the former president of the United States, was successful in achieving his presidency mostly because he shared similarities with the African American members of the country. Besides focusing on the physical similarities between them, he would also talk about the struggles they faced since he could, to a certain extent, understand them and relate. Hence rose his popularity amongst that segment of the country, ultimately helping him win the election.

. . .

Some additional ways in which you can persuade people by using verbal and non-verbal **powers of language** include:

- Using affirmative words
- Engaging with them
- Maintaining eye contact
- Connecting emotionally
- Flattery
- Using a bit of hyperbole
- Getting personal
- Using emotional language

Tap into the power of language and use affirmative words like 'definitely,' 'most,' 'do this,' 'be that' instead of 'maybe' 'I guess.' Make sure your tone is firm and positive. Be respectful and kind at all times. Also, use urgent words like 'today,' 'currently,' 'now' that reflects earnestness and scarcity; this would drive individuals to make a decision quickly because the products are running out.

Additionally, people are more likely to be persuaded when you tell a story, ask them questions, share personal stories, find mutual interests and similarities, and engage with them. This not only helps you understand them better but also makes them more receptive to persuasion. Eye contact allows you to build rapport, provided that it's consistent and not too prolonged – the latter's just creepy. Add a happy smile and some charm to the mix, and persuading people will be a piece of cake. Maintaining eye contact is an easy and super subtle way of influencing individuals to get them to do what you want. Complementing the person by saying things like, "Someone of your caliber deserves better", "This product would suit your beautiful face structure," or by stating an opinion as fact, and using language like 'fantastic' 'stunning' can also go a long way. It helps if you get more personal and use 'I' and 'we' in your sentences. Many times, persuasive language involves many loaded words and images; all-natural, homegrown, organic, new and improved – it's an endless list. They shouldn't be forced and your pitch or speech shouldn't sound robotic. The trick is to build a connection with the individual, leave them charmed, and have a positive effect on them. In very subtle ways, this would influence their decision making.

ONE LAST SUPER helpful persuasive tactic we can add in this section is to prefer **emotion** over logic. Our brain's cognitive and emotional pathways are independent and run parallel to one another. If you've ever felt strongly about something despite knowing how illogical it is, you'll know what we're talking about. Our emotional pathways are stronger and more intuitive; rationality follows much later. If you really want people to be persuaded, figure them out and tap into their emotional responses. We are emotional beings before we are logical beings, hence making this tactic extremely effective. Appeal to their emotional side rather than their logical one because that would enhance your likelihood of successful persuasion. This persuasion tactic is what most people in politics also tend to use by telling people of the community to vote for them for the 'good of the country,' or paint a picture of the country in shambles and without stating facts but focusing on hyperbole language to sway the voters' minds.

Basic Persuasion Skills You Can Use

When it comes to persuading individuals in your everyday life, there are also some other easy techniques that you can use for effective results. CEOs, politicians, and other leaders regularly use these subtle techniques to get what they want, and most people don't even realize how they are being persuaded. Perfecting these techniques will need practice, but they are simple to follow.

SOME OF THESE basic persuasion skills include building trust among the individuals you wish to persuade before you begin your pitch or argument. As we will discuss in the next section, Aristotle was the first one to recognize that logic is not the only thing that persuades individuals. Emotion is equally, if not more, important. One of the ways to build trust is to find common ground and identify shared values or thoughts between your audience and yourself. Commonality can truly have a profound, subtle impact on your likeability and persuasiveness.

ADDITIONALLY, building empathy is also equally as important. As we mentioned earlier, emotions are the best thing to use to your advantage when it comes to persuasion. Hence, listen to the other side and understand where they are coming from. Once you do, it will be easier to convince them to believe and follow your viewpoint. Similarly, try not to exaggerate your stories and beliefs or use hyperbole language to paint a more pronounced version of your argument. Getting too unnecessarily emotional or faking your emotions is not recommended. This will neither build trust nor empathy because once a lie or discrepancy is spotted, your entire argument will fall apart, and persuasion will be much more difficult, maybe even impossible.

WHEN PRESENTING your case and argument, think carefully about the content and what you have to say. Build your case from the bottom up by presenting the problems and needs first and then a logical and practical solution to them. People would listen to others when it is serving their interest or at least relates to them. Otherwise, they are likely to not even listen to what you have to say.

THUS SPEND time to study your audience and see if they need to be persuaded and whether the argument you are about to make is relevant and important to them. For example, if you want to persuade an individual to buy your car, but they don't even have a license or know how to drive, then persuading them would be futile. However, sometimes this becomes difficult if you are pitching your argument or aiming to persuade a complete stranger. In this case, having a strong introduction makes all the difference. Perhaps having an acquaintance to introduce you would also be helpful. But either way, during introductions, is where excellent communication skills become extremely important.

ONE OF THE ways to effectively communicate in order to persuade them to buy your product or service or to follow your argument or stance is to listen to the other side first. This will also provide you with information about who they are, what their values and preferences are. With this information you gather, you can create a personalized pitch that is likely to be more effective at persuasion. When you think about it, this is exactly what politicians also do. They come to meet you and ask you questions and listen to your needs and problems first and then create a pitch that contains their policies and how they can fulfill your need or fix your problems once you vote for them. Doing this also makes the other person believe that they are being valued and heard, which is another advantage that contributes to persuasiveness. It is a subtle way of increasing their likeability and making the individual likely to be persuaded.

FOR EFFECTIVE PERSUASION, present your pitch and argument with few good reasons. By having too many arguments or reasons, you are likely to confuse and overwhelm your audience. Not only that, but it will also dilute the impact of the aforementioned reasons you used. Hence, it's always good to start with and stick to two to three strong reasons to support your stance or argument. If needed, and when the conversation progresses, you can increase and add more points.

AS WE HAVE ALREADY POINTED out, persuasion often involves arguments. Two sides are presented, and so it is important for you to be agreeable with the other side even if you don't necessarily agree with it. This will tell them that you are respectful and open-minded. If you don't do that and refute what they say, they will be slightly cold to you and dismiss your arguments as well. Of course, by agreeing with everything they say, you won't be able to effectively persuade them. Therefore, it's best if you have an agreeable attitude and respectfully and logically counter their argument, and acknowledge the reasoning behind their choices.

THOUGH BEING confident is not exactly a persuasive technique, it surely helps to subtly influence others to listen to your point of view and sway their minds. Whatever you pitch, make sure you have confidence in it. If you yourself don't believe or are not committed to the argument or pitch, the audience will never be persuaded. Your unbridled sense of certainty and natural confidence can be the key to convincing others. This is also what lawyers commonly do; they may even fake their confidence to get the judge or jury to believe their pitch. Even if it is something they themselves don't necessarily support or believe, lawyers and attorneys will stay firm in their stance and influence others in order to persuade them.

ABOVE ALL, it is important for you to be subtle and covert with all of these persuasion techniques in order to be successful in delivering your pitch and getting others to do what you want them to do when it comes to daily tasks and living. Simply saying 'Believe me' or blatantly presenting your argument will not help your claim or persuade them. Be patient and communicate subtly. Perfecting the art of persuasion involves patience and commitment.

Factors to Consider Before Persuading Someone

Now that you are fully equipped with all the types of tactics and techniques you can use to persuade individuals and get them to do what you want, it is also important to take into consideration certain important factors.

THESE PERSUASION TACTICS will come in handy in your everyday lives, whether it is in a professional, social, or intimate setting.

PERSUASION IS TRULY an art for people who have fully mastered it. To some, having a knack for convincing people to do what you want comes naturally; but for others, consistent and frequent practice is required. Before you go ahead and put your learning to the test, here are some of the factors you should consider that will help you in finding individuals who would be easy targets to persuade:

- **Assess How Easy it Will Be to Persuade a Particular Person**

If you already have a target in mind who you want to persuade, try to get a feel of who they are. Not only will this help you to be more empathetic and build a connection with them, but it will also give you an idea of how difficult or easy it would be to persuade them and how much effort is required. There are several factors that can help you identify this, for example, how much interest they show in interacting with you, their demeanor if they are bored, and other nonverbal communication cues we discussed earlier.

- **Group Membership**

Another important factor to consider is the group that your targeted individuals belong to, and if they in any way may be against what you are trying to persuade them to do. Individuals who belong to certain groups will be less likely to go against what the group follows, thus making your efforts of convincing futile. Their loyalty to the group precedes what you have to say. On the other hand, if what you have to say is congruent to their group values, it would become very easy to persuade them.

- **Assess the Level of Self Esteem Someone Has**

Research shows that individuals who have low self-esteem tend to be easily persuaded. This is because they are likely to value other's opinions of others than their own and have low confidence in themselves. Finding someone of such a nature would thus make your job of persuasion much easier. However, the real challenge comes in figuring out the level of self-esteem the individual has. In these cases, observing their nonverbal communication skills and body language would be quite useful. For example, as we discussed earlier, notice whether their posture is slouched or confident if they are making eye contact with you, and check whether if they are agreeing to what you are saying, such as by nodding their head.

- **Inhibition of Aggression**

Before beginning your pitch or requesting your favor, it would also be helpful to figure out the level of aggression displayed by the targeted individual. Those who seem to have a cool head and do not show any aggression tend to be persuaded much easier than aggressive individuals. This is because they won't challenge what the persuader is saying and would just listen. Even if they are made to feel uncomfortable, if they lack aggression, you would still be able to influence their decision. Therefore, it is helpful to find individuals who don't tend to be aggressive if you want to successfully get them to do what you want.

- **If the Individual Displays Depressive Tendencies**

If the targeted individual who you want to persuade displays depressive tendencies, persuading them might be easy. This is because they tend to again, value other people's opinions, more than their own, and they also have higher agreeability. These individuals have both an inhibition of aggression and low self-esteem, making them ideal candidates for persuasion. However, it might also be the case that depressive individuals are not exactly persuaded by you but are only agreeing with you so that they are left alone and don't have any energy to argue.

- **If the Individual Feels Socially Inadequate**

Some individuals tend to view themselves as socially inadequate because they believe they are incompetent, not good enough, lack skills, and whatnot. They, therefore, lose confidence in their ability to continue conversations or argue. These types of individuals can thus be easily persuaded because they will let you continue talking and would even feel compelled to listen to you. You can identify whether an individual feels socially inept by the way they make conversations, such as whether they lead conversations, are talkative, their tone, and their body language.

The Aristotelian Theories of Persuasion

Here, we'd like to tell you about the Aristotelian elements of persuasive arguments, which include ethos, logos, and pathos. *Ethos* is an appeal to expertise or authority. A lawyer's word on legal matters is more persuasive than a doctor's, whereas a doctor's word is more compelling on medical issues than a lawyer's. Hence when individuals believe and trust your word, they will buy your ideas. In order to be persuasive, ethos states that the individual must demonstrate that they have the knowledge, skills, and character to be able to convince others effectively.

SIMILARLY, *logos* is an appeal to logic, cognition, and facts; as the name suggests, it depends on reason and accurate information put forward. The appeal of logos is aimed at appealing to the rational and logical part of an individual. For example, some people can be persuaded when facts and figures are presented to them, and so when there is no sound explanation or concrete information supporting your appeal, it is not logos and will not be persuasive. Another great example is scientific studies used as arguments.

FINALLY, *pathos,* unlike logos, *is* an appeal to motivations, feelings, and sentiments; they have nothing to do with cognition, figures, or facts. Using emotions to persuade others and elicit emotions from them to get them to do what you want them to do. It's all about winning their hearts. Getting people to feel happy, sad, or angry to support your argument is perhaps the most potent persuasive tactic you can use of all three. The best way to do this is by creating imaginative, descriptive, and elaborate stories and vivid examples to bring your persuasive argument to life.

The Six Principles of Influence

On the note of experts on rhetoric and persuasion, Robert Cialdini, a psychologist, suggested six principles of influence. These are:

- Reciprocity
- Authority
- Scarcity
- Consistency
- Liking

Applying these principles will help you build stronger, long-term relationships *ethically.* We've already discussed how powerful a tool reciprocity is when it comes to persuading other people. The next on the list is **authority**, which is similar to Aristotle's *ethos.* People who are more knowledgeable and carry expert credibility are more likely to persuade a lot of people. They do this by gaining people's trust: when we trust people, we're more easily swayed by them. Again, businesses do this all the time. It's easier to sell cosmetic toothpaste when you put it in the hands of a dentist. People will be persuaded more when you sign your emails with a signature of qualification. If we were honest, appeal to authority is perhaps the most genuine form of persuasion, but very few people use it. That's because people assume that everyone that they talk to will automatically know their authority. If you want to convince more people, make sure you tell them your credentials, display them on social media or at the workplace, and make sure you also *sound* authoritative. Of course, putting your life story on full display isn't always going to be an option, especially in casual conversations – for that, you can convey your expertise through a handful of short anecdotes.

NEXT ON THE list is **scarcity**, which means that the less you have of one thing, the more you crave it. This is basic supply and demand. Businesses do this by restricting their products by time and collection. Certain clothes will only be available at certain times of the year. There's a sale but only for the next 15 days. This creates a sense of urgency, which influences a person's decision-making. Dark Triad personalities do this by using the *breadcrumbing* technique, where they offer love and affection in scarcity – *that's* manipulative. Generally, as long as the scarcity isn't created over basic needs like love or shelter and security, it only adds value to what's scarce. One thing to remember here would be to focus less on the sense of loss and more on gain – there is *value* to what's scarce.

NEXT ON THE list is **consistency**. People will hear what you have to say if you follow through. Make a plan. Commit to it. Tell people you followed through. Take accountability for it publically. People love consistency. They're persuaded heavily by someone who can keep their word. Finally, it's easy to convince people when the person talking is **likable** and relatable. People listen to their friends, peers, and family; it's a relatively simple idea. Social cues are essential for all of us; they help us see, think and feel what everyone around us is seeing, thinking, and feeling. All of us instinctively want to belong and feel the need to be liked by the people around us. We want a common ground with people and connect with them, and when we do, we tend to do what those people are doing. Getting in someone's good books is a great way to persuade people, and you can do this either by finding common ground to connect with them or approaching them with *genuine* praise. You can use this technique to build rapport, trust, and connect with people, but make sure you don't overdo it and end up buttering them instead – remember, if it's not genuine, you're most likely manipulating them.

PRACTICING these six principles of influence will enable you to make the most of your knowledge about persuasion and get people to do what you want. Fair warning, though, *don't* use these skills to control and manipulate people. Dark psychology and Dark Triad make use of the same sources, but their intentions are malicious – as long as yours are authentic and genuine, you're good to go.

Is Persuasion Moral?

Right now, you're probably thinking: is all of this even moral? There's a lot of debate on whether using persuasive tactics is ethical or not. Not all persuasion is ethical; we'll admit that. But, not all of it is unethical. To ask if persuasion is ethical or not is the same as asking if using a knife is ethical or not – it depends on *how* you use it. Using your knife to cut butter and using it to hurt someone are two different things – it's the same with persuasion tactics. It matters who you're using it on, whether you're in a position of power over them, whether you're using it to brainwash or torture someone, and so on.

THE GOOD THING IS, you're not the first person to wonder that. Researchers have put two tests to establish if a persuasive tactic is ethical or not: The TARES test and the Fitzpatrick and Gauthier Test.

THE **TARES** TEST has the following five markers: the truthfulness of the message being conveyed, the speaker's authenticity, the respect for the audience, the equity of the appeal, and social responsibility. Ask the following about a persuasive tactic:

- Does the tactic involve lying or truth by omission?
- Would you personally like it if someone else were to say the same words to you?
- Is the person you're persuading free to opt out of what you're offering?
- Do you feel good about being involved in this act?
- Does this persuasive tactic create a negative space for other people who are not directly involved?

On the other hand, the **Fitzpatrick and Gauthier test** has the following three markers: the purpose of the persuasion, the consequences it will create, and the level of interference in the decision-making process.

. . .

PERSUASION DOESN'T INVOLVE enforcement or any underhanded techniques. It gives the person on the receiving end the option to opt out of buying what you're selling. Plus, unlike the dark triad, you're connecting with them on an emotional level and actually know what they want.

To SUM both of these tests up, for a persuasive tactic to be ethical, it has to take into account:

- Both the parties' perspective and intentions
- The positive and negative consequences of the action
- The will of the person on the receiving end

If the persuasive tactic lacks that, it's unethical. If the persuasive tactics fail the tests mentioned above, they're likely being used for coercion, brainwashing, exploitation, or personal gains.

The Fine Line Between Persuasion & Manipulation

By now, you might also be wondering what the difference between persuasion and manipulation is since the two sound so similar. The end goal of both is to get people to do what you want them to do, so how do you differentiate between manipulation and persuasion?

WELL, the difference between the two and the fine line drawn between them is simply the intent behind the behaviors. Persuasion tends to have more positive intent, for example, to benefit the individual who is being persuaded. However, manipulation more or less has to do with fooling an individual to exert control over them so that they listen, buy, or do what you want them to. This does not necessarily serve benefits to the person being manipulated but rather to the manipulator. In fact, it is likely that in the case of manipulation, the person being manipulated is also being harmed or will experience a loss of sorts. This loss can be emotional, material, or financial. In manipulation, the greater benefit is being served to the manipulator rather than the person being manipulated, while the same cannot be said about persuasion. At the very least, in persuasion, the persuader is not *willingly* causing harm to the person they are persuading.

THE BEST WAY TO explain the difference between persuasion and manipulation is through an example of a car dealership. Suppose a family of six comes to the dealership looking for a suitable and affordable mini-van. However, the salesperson uses all his persuasion techniques to convince the family to buy a two-seater convertible instead because it's trendier, looks good, and will enable the parents to reclaim their youth. The salesperson is adamant that they buy the convertible simply because it has a higher commission. This thus cannot be considered persuasion but rather manipulation because it is serving the benefit of the manipulator and not exactly the other person at the end of the conversation.

SIMILARLY, if a tobacco company states that it sells its products to allow individuals to "enjoy their lives," well, that's manipulations because it's clearly not true.

THEREFORE, when persuasion skills are used to benefit an individual at the end of the conversation, it is likely to be persuasion. However, the opposite will thus be considered manipulation. It is the net benefit for both parties, all parties; the intent behind the action, and the truthfulness of the process, help to distinguish persuasion and manipulation.

Professional Traits

Though generally in life, using manipulative tactics and techniques to influence others is common. This tends to become more profound in professional settings when money, power, and recognition are involved.

MANIPULATORS TEND TO use subtle ways of influencing managers, coworkers, the community, and the system itself to meet their own needs and personal agenda. They take years to hone these skills, and sometimes it is even part of their studies and training.

PROFESSIONAL TASKS REQUIRE a person to exhibit certain personality traits to get the job done by their nature and succeed at their job. This, more often than not, tends to result in competitiveness amongst workers, which becomes more pronounced for those fitting the dark triad personality. They may covertly and subtly use manipulation, lying, and blackmail to get ahead of their counterparts.

IN FACT, for some professions, using dark psychology tactics is the only way to excel. Whether that is manipulating their coworkers, clients, or members of the community, these professions use tactics to persuade or influence others.

. . .

A FEW OF such professions that utilize characteristics that are in common with the dark triad include attorneys, politicians, public speakers, marketers, and salespeople.

THERE ARE several Dark Psychology techniques that people use to self-promote and step up the ladder in their careers or to get people to do what they want. Here's a closer look at each of these professions and how they use the Dark Psychology techniques we had discussed earlier.

Salespeople and Marketers

Salespeople and Marketers have long understood that to sell a product or service, they must tap into their potential customers' psychology. Salespeople will sell a product or service to you by influencing you; even if you want to say no, they might continue to be persistent and use tactics such as telling you how much you need what they are selling. Perhaps by using emotion, they may tell you that a specific product or service will help improve your life and relationships. Emotional language is an integral part of pitching a product or service to people.

AS WE MENTIONED EARLIER, our emotional pathways are much stronger than logical ones. Hence these people tend to use a number of tactics and techniques designed to persuade customers by making them emotional. They follow a model of 'what's in it for me' and thus design their sales pitches around what the consumer will get out of buying their product or service.

. . .

FOR INSTANCE, they are more likely to tell you how a particular product or service is likely to benefit you rather than describe its features, specifications, and how exactly to use it. They will talk about how you need their certain product or service, how your life is incomplete without it, how it will make you happier and your life easier. And they will do their best to make you believe it.

SALESPEOPLE TEND to be individuals who are trained to be influential; in the way they talk, how they dress, their mannerisms, and whatnot. In all these covert ways, they influence individuals and often intimidate them to persuade them to buy what they are selling.

TO GET TO THE TOP, salespeople will impose their authority and appear extremely credible to potential customers. In fact, companies hire people who seem naturally likable, approachable, and amiable. Think about the number of times you have seen celebrities endorse a certain product. Or think about how companies use credible individuals like dentists to endorse toothpaste.

MORE OFTEN THAN NOT, salespeople also tend to be good-looking and attractive. One of the tactics they then use is to be warm and friendly towards potential customers to build a connection with them, perhaps by finding common ground. This is what they start by and then slowly move towards appealing to their emotions through the product or service.

. . .

WHEN IT COMES TO MARKETERS, they, too, use the same tactics to attract customers to the product or service they are advertising. Their advertisements tend to display how life is incomplete or imperfect without a specific product or service. These advertisements also display how it can fulfill a need in an individual's life, one that you perhaps never even considered or thought about. All in all, their job is to make you want something by creating advertisements, and manipulate your emotions, thought processes, and decision-making abilities. Their entire job is to sway your minds and influence your behavior.

Politicians

Politics is not just an art but also a science. Political psychology falls into the realm of Dark Psychology. It is the one area where this field of study thrives. Politics uses the learning from Dark Psychology to frame one's opponent, influence voter decisions, and make the community favor collective benefit rather than individualistic benefit through behaviors. They use persuasion tactics to frame their opponent as being incompetent, the state as being hopeless, frame themselves as being the person who can fix the problems, and more.

ONCE THESE LEADERS actually come into power, they then frame their government as being effective and excellent and find someone to blame when things don't go well. Furthermore, some leaders may even be so extreme so as to instill extremist and religious beliefs in their followers and manipulate them to do things they don't want to do.

LEADERS AND POLITICIANS strategically use a myriad of clever persuasion tactics to persuade the public to like and vote for them, even if it may not be in the public's best interest. Politicians are greedy for power, and their entire success depends on the willingness of the public to follow them. They also tend to be charming, supportive, good-looking, and overall meant to have a lasting impression on others. In fact, a successful politician and leader is anyone who can charm people at will.

NOT ONLY THAT, but they also tend to be more likely to possess all the dark psychology traits we mentioned earlier. In particular, they would have an inflated sense of self, a sensitive ego, spiteful nature, and a belief that they are entitled to special treatment. They interact with the public to show affection and give their validation, something that individuals naturally crave, particularly from those in superior positions. As we discussed earlier, manipulators would also engage in insincere flattery to get in the good books of people. This tactic is what leaders and politicians also do to have the public support their party or policies.

FURTHERMORE, politicians also try as much as they can to make the public believe that they are just like them. An individual is more likely to vote for a leader who they can relate to; this can be in terms of physical appearance, ideals, preferences, and whatnot. For example, George Bush is considered to be a political genius who used several covert manipulations to persuade the American public. One of these included fitting into the average American stereotype. He was considered to be the 'All-American president,' which made him an even more desirable leader.

. . .

AT THE SAME TIME, they also make sure that they continue to be friendly and approachable. This allows the public to believe that the politician is in it for the greater good and people, but really it's just a form of covert manipulation.

ONE OF THE most popular dark psychology traits used by Politicians included appealing to the emotions of the public. They do this by creating a sense of in-group versus out-group situation, which incites anger, rage, and outrage amongst the public and encourages them to vote. Since our emotions are the dominant force for decision-making, it is this that politicians most frequently use. Therefore, instead of discussing rational policies, they are more likely to promote national pride in their speeches, using phrases like, 'our great country,' 'what our country stands for,' and 'how we have to serve our nation.'

THE 'WHAT'S in it for me' model that we discussed in the salespeople and marketers section also applies to politicians who also use it in their speeches. Human beings inherently look for things that are of interest to them and would fulfill their need. However, when you rationally think about it, there is very little in it for the public. For the most part, one's individual vote amounts to nothing, and if they partake in war, they might lose their lives. So what's the good that would come out of voting for a politician?

DUE TO THIS REASON, politicians use what's known as political persuasion. They will prevent people from thinking about what rationally is in it for them but focus on 'serving the motherland.' Additionally, the ideals of honesty, integrity, national loyalty, and responsibility will be exaggerated and promoted by them. Gradually, the group starts becoming more important than the self. However, this way of thinking tends to serve the benefit of the political leader more than the country itself.

MOREOVER, they would also be more inclined towards being Machiavellian. After all, the Machiavelli theory came into being through politics, to begin with. Most right-wing politicians use the principles of this theory in their speeches and actions. Politicians want to get to the top and succeed, and they will not care about how they do it as long as they do.

Attorneys

Lawyers and attorneys are known to be extremely convincing and firm in their stances. After all, they earn their living by persuading individuals, whether it is the judge or jury who needs to be persuaded. Lawyers have become synonymous with persuasive and manipulative. Winning a case is more important for most attorneys than justice. Any excellent attorney can alter reality and make the jury believe what they want them to believe. They change reality by planting false memories in the judge or jury, for example, by making them believe that their memory is not as accurate as they think it is.

HENCE, lawyers and attorneys are abundantly trained at the art of persuasion, besides legal analytical skills. So much so that they can construct false memories and convince others to believe it happened. In fact, they may event taint the past memories in their memories. For lawyers and attorneys, manipulating evidence and reality is often what they have to do in order to win their case.

. . .

THUS, naturally, their training and studies also include adopting dark psychology traits so that individuals believe what they tell them and follow their stance. Regardless of their personal and moral beliefs, they will make you believe what they want you to believe.

ATTORNEYS TEND TO BE AUTHORITATIVE, loud, and confident. Whether they are morally right or wrong does not matter as long as they can successfully convince individuals to believe them. For that reason, they employ the tactic of appealing to the emotions of the jury or judge. For example, in the case of a murder trial, the chances are that attorneys would more likely discuss the impact of the murder on the victim's families and the mental and emotional repercussions rather than what actually happened because the emotions attached to the murder are more impactful than the facts. In other words, the emotional impact would triumph the logical details of the case and influence decision making.

MOREOVER, attorneys also use what's known as 'covert advocacy,' which refers to all the covert and unconscious ways they impact the jury's decision-making. These covert advocacy techniques can be reflected in their authoritative style of dressing, how they talk, how they may distort evidence to influence perception, and much more.

BESIDES PERSUADING and manipulating the judge and jury, lawyers are also trained at persuading their clients to believe them. They must exhibit their expertise and experience in the relevant field in order to get clients to trust them and sign them on.

It's no doubt that attorneys and lawyers, to a certain degree, possess qualities of the Dark Triad; it is what determines their success at cases. The more lack of empathy they have, the more impartial and successful they can be as attorneys.

THE USE of hyperbole and emotional language is widespread in law settings, as the attorneys try to emotionally influence the jury's decision. For that reason, they may exaggerate details as well. In some ways, they twist reality to change the jury's perception towards the attorney's client.

Law Enforcement

In everyday interactions, law enforcement, like the police, has to constantly communicate with individuals and the wider public and gain their compliance when needed. They exert their authority when necessary, making them the prime example of the Dark Triad.

TIME AND AGAIN, we have seen multiple cases of law enforcement unfairly using their power and authority over community members simply because they can. There are also some subtle techniques used by law enforcement to influence people without them even realizing it. For example, with their rigid and authoritative demeanor, how they communicate,

ON THE FLIP SIDE, when dealing with conflict or an uncooperative individual, law enforcement may need to use covert techniques of persuasion as well to coerce them. In terms of posture, gestures, tone of their voice, and eye contact, their nonverbal communication exudes authority and confidence, which in itself brings about compliance in people.

Investigation

When it comes to investigations, whether in police offices or courtrooms, there is extensive training involved. Making people believe you enough to share the truth with you or make a confession requires learning a number of covert persuasion techniques. Investigators need to be authoritative and amiable while still maintaining a considerable distance.

THEY NEED to be approachable enough to encourage others to share information, yet they also have to be rigid and not show any empathy or remorse. Thus it may take years to perfect this art. More often than not, investigators have to investigate suspects who tend to match the dark triad and could thus be psychopaths, sociopaths, or narcissists. To elicit information, confessions and catch the culprit, they will have to tap into such people's psyches. Hence dark psychology is a major part of their study. They must discover whether a suspect fits into the dark triad or not based on their behaviors and actions.

AT THE SAME TIME, investigations and interrogations are notorious for eliciting false confessions as well. Some investigators can be so persuasive as to plant false memories and make individuals believe something they didn't do. This is where dark psychology also comes in.

. . .

SOME OF THE dark psychology tactics they use are hyperbole and emotional language, which appeals to an individual's emotional side. For example, talking about the impact of the victim's actions on their families, how they would feel, and whatnot. By exaggerating emotions, interrogators can be successful at eliciting confessions and information, whether true or false. Additionally, they also excessively guilt trip the individual to elicit information, again by exaggerating details and emotions and using hyperbole.

Civil Rights

Civil rights involve protecting the rights and freedom of members of a country from the government, social organizations, and private entities. They also ensure equal and complete participation of an individual in civil matters. For example, having the right to free speech, equal pay, and voting. This obviously entails forming a group that has a common leader. These leaders can use certain persuasive tactics to exert their control. Some of these can include stoking anger amongst the group against a common enemy, for example, the government. This increases the group's cohesion and power. However, all the while, it is likely that these civil rights leaders simultaneously try to reduce the power of their followers' powers and independence.

CIVIL RIGHTS LEADERS are constantly persuading the public to help push their narratives and personal agendas. In some ways, this persuasion can also often be thought of as covert manipulation. Much like politicians, these civil rights movements also focus on making an impact through the in-group and out-group technique. For example, by convincing the public that the government is against them and it does not have their best interest at heart. These leaders exaggerate this problem to a greater extent, making the group believe that this is a huge problem and the leader and civil rights group will be the solution to their problem. They would also cut out any other opposing opinions that may bring doubt in the minds of the followers. This is done by calling these opinions 'idiotic,' 'manipulative,' and 'slander.'

IT CREATES a sense of them versus us environment, and this is what fuels their protest. It also increases their anger, rage, emotions, all of which channeled through their protests.

TAKE the example of the women's movements in the 1970s. This too was a form of civil rights, and the leaders persuaded the women to fight for themselves and fight against the government. By having a common enemy, their unity was solidified, and their narrative for equality was pushed forward.

AGAIN, civil rights leaders use the ever so common tactics of manipulators, which include playing to the emotions of the public and using hyperbole. By enraging the public and making them emotional, civil rights leaders succeed in their movements. They also exaggerate emotions and situations to appeal to the public and thus use hyperbole.

MUCH LIKE POLITICIANS, most civil rights leaders also tend to be charismatic, loud, and passionate. But unlike politicians, they are better at making the public believe that they are similar to them. A civil rights leader truly fights for the community, and so they can influence a large group of people easily. Whatever they do is for the good of the community, and so they can make the public trust and follow them. However, civil rights movements all include a selfish narrative. Each person fights for their own benefit, to fulfill their own need, or to gain an advantage.

Columnists or Writers

Columnists are reporters who write about real-time events and present their opinions on them or share their general stances on a particular subject. All of this is done with the aim to sway the readers to believe in what they have to say. The same can be said about writers who also use writing to manipulate stories and characters to create a reality for readers for them to believe in.

IN A LOT OF WAYS, one might argue that the job of a writer or columnist is to persuade and manipulate. They produce pieces to convince their readers to believe and follow their narrative and opinion. For columnists and writers, their opinion is the right one, and they want everyone to agree and believe in it as well. They use affirmative language and strong words to show how their opinions are actually facts. Moreover, this is where the popular form of persuasive writing also came into fruition. Writers are taught the art of forming sentences and use words that aim to make readers believe in their stance.

MANIPULATING the readers is a very powerful tool and one that can have a deep impact. Each sentence is carefully written with specific language by a columnist and, in subconscious ways, can have a profound impact on the reader without them realizing it. That is why most political stances are written and shared down to encourage discourse and sway the reader's opinions.

WRITERS AND COLUMNISTS attempt to change people's minds or make them form opinions about things they had no preconceived notions about. Due to that reason, dark psychology tricks and techniques are extensively used to make an impact and influence opinions.

THEY MAKE the readers feel like they can relate to the writer and what they have written, for example, by making them believe that the two have a common goal. They tap into the emotions of the readers as well to covertly influence their opinion. This is the most powerful tool of persuasion that columnists and writers use the most. For example, when writing about a political stance, they are more likely to talk about the negative repercussions of a group they don't support rather than stating the facts and figures. They know that this approach is more likely to elicit support and favorable decisions rather than presenting rational and logical information.

Doctors and Therapists

Any profession that extensively deals with people and involves heaps of communication is bound to be manipulative and persuasive. Doctors and therapists tend to communicate with patients on a regular basis. The two work together to solve a patient's problem and devise a treatment plan.

IT CAN BE hard to believe how therapists and doctors can manipulate or persuade individuals, but they do. Of course, not all of it is with malicious intent. Sometimes, doctors can influence their patients' opinions simply because they are the authority figure and hold all the expertise and power. For example, if a patient goes to the doctor because they are experiencing a stomach ache, they will likely take whatever medication or treatment the doctor suggests because they are the ones who know better. Similarly, this power can be used to persuade individuals quite easily. If a patient is not willing to go through with treatment or therapy, doctors can persuade them and make them change their mind.

WHEN IT COMES TO THERAPISTS, they have comprehensively studied psychology and dark psychology in order to be able to deal with all kinds of clients. Hence they are well aware of the dark triad and related personality traits they possess and the tactics they use. Most therapists have to deal with narcissists, psychopaths, and sociopaths, so they must be aware of how they interact in order to be able to diagnose and treat them or handle their outbursts.

THERAPISTS MUST BE aware of manipulative clients so as not to fall for their tricks and be able to identify their tactics effectively. Moreover, they are the only ones who can treat and manage individuals who have chronic manipulative tendencies. The therapist would work with them to identify unhealthy and manipulative behavioral patterns and make the client understand how that is toxic and harmful for them and those around them.

THOUGH CONSIDERED COMPLETELY UNETHICAL, therapists can easily manipulate and influence the opinions of their clients as well. Again, therapists are someone who has the upper hand since they are more knowledgeable than the client. In some cases, what they suggest becomes the opinion of their client. The client has come to the therapist because they have in some ways lost some control in their lives and need to regain it somehow. The therapist can manipulate the client to help them on their path to self-discovery and improved mental well-being. This is manipulation that is ethical, as it is serving the good of the client. However, when this power is misused, it can be highly unethical and unacceptable.

SUMMARY

Here's a summary of everything we learned in this chapter:

- Persuasion is the art of convincing individuals to perform an action that would benefit them, and the persuader
- There is a big difference between persuasion and manipulation, as the latter only benefits the manipulator
- There are a number of approaches and persuasion tactics you can use to get people to do what you want, for example, by using empathy, emotions, or authority
- There are some factors you should consider before persuading someone, for example, what their personality and circumstances are, and more
- We also discussed the theories surrounding persuasion and whether persuasion is moral or not
- There are certain professions that employ persuasion techniques more than others, such as writers, politicians, and lawyers

5
BRINGING IT ALL TOGETHER

By now, we can understand that manipulators, psychopaths, sociopaths, Machiavellians, and narcissists are not villains that we see in movies. They walk amongst us, and we do interact with them every now and then. They probably appear as normal friends, family members, acquaintances, and colleagues, but sooner or later, they will reveal their true colors, and it won't take long.

IT LIES on you to recognize and identify their manipulative tricks and tactics and not fall for them. After reading everything about Dark Psychology in this book, you are likely to spot their behaviors. Though you may regard successful CEOs, politicians, and business leaders as geniuses, we can still learn a few things from them. By learning their tactics, we can persuade others to get what we want. However, it is imperative to note that there is a fine line between persuasion and manipulation. Ethics and honesty are what divides the two. It is okay to persuade someone to believe your opinion or do what you want them to do, yet it is completely unethical to blackmail or manipulate them without them knowing or not. Or when there is no real benefit for them.

Persuasion can be a great gift if it's done with the right intentions. It can galvanize change, bring people together, and push progress forward towards better things. And more importantly, it will help you reach your goals of influencing individuals. To get people to do what you want, you will need to practice all of these tactics for a while. Persuasion is a skill that can only be perfected through experience and practice. Just like politicians, salespeople, and attorneys all train themselves in the art, you will also need to do the same.

Without proper ways to persuade people, we would essentially be handicapped in life and not be able to enjoy so many life pleasures. For example, we would not be able to properly negotiate deals on the house or cars we buy or be able to progress in our career as efficiently and take the next step in our intimate relationships. Moreover, you might also find yourself to be too gullible, able to fall for so many scams and tricks, and not be able to make smart decisions. In these cases, being equipped with all the tactics that we discussed earlier would significantly improve our lives and decrease our susceptibility to falling for tricksters. Hence, in a lot of ways, persuasion is a life skill that should be taught to all individuals because it reduces the individual's vulnerability to be scammed and deceived.

Dark Psychology states that we all have a dark side within us and fall on a continuum of malicious and evil acts. But what differentiates us from the criminals we see in police stations are our moral compass and the ability to act on these impulses. So while we may be aware of the ways to deceive people, it is highly important not to take advantage of this. When it comes to harming an individual in any way, then that is where you should draw the line.

BY EMPLOYING the NLP skills we studied, you can easily observe influential individuals to learn from them. Look up videos or observe somebody who you know is good at persuasion; identify what makes them charismatic, what kind of body language they use, how they communicate, and how they carry themselves. Then, start working on yourself. Employ the skills you notice in them, and practice in front of a mirror. Remember the key takeaways from this book that will give you the power to persuade. By doing all of this, you will certainly become a master persuader.

IN THIS BOOK, we hope you have learned a considerable amount about what makes CEOs and politicians so successful and how you can emulate their qualities to up your game and excel in your professional and personal lives. Faking charisma, empathy, and your overall verbal and nonverbal is extremely easy if you want to influence other people. Of course, you will need to focus on every aspect of yourself, but as we've learned, all of this can become effortless after practicing.

NOW IS the time to put your learning in full gear and practice like there's no tomorrow. Eventually, you will definitely be able to easily get people to do what you want!